Guide to
HAWAIIAN REEF FISHES

John E. Randall

Senior Ichthyologist
Bernice Pauahi Bishop Museum
Honolulu, Hawaii

Harrowood Books

HARROWOOD BOOKS
3943 North Providence Road
Newtown Square, PA 19073

copublished and distributed in Hawaii by
TREASURES OF NATURE
P.O. Box 195, Kaneohe, HI 96744

Library of Congress Cataloging in Publication Data

Randall, John E.   1924—
    Guide to Hawaiian reef fishes
 	
    Includes Index
    1. Marine fishes—Hawaii—Identification.
2. Coral reef fauna—Hawaii—Identification.
3. Fishes— Identification.   4. Fishes—Hawaii—
Identification.   I. Title.
QL636.5.H3R358   1985   597.092'59   85-24551
ISBN 0-915180-29-4 (Paper edition)

ISBN 0-915180-07-3 (cloth)   321
ISBN 0-915180-02-2 (plastic)

CONTENTS

Chart of a Fish

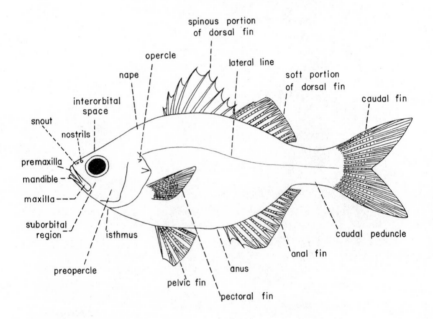

INTRODUCTION

The primary purpose of this book is to provide for the identification of the reef fishes an observer is most apt to see when snorkeling or SCUBA diving in Hawaiian waters. A plastic edition of the color plates from this volume is available. It can be taken to the sea shore, in an open boat, or even underwater if desired.

A total of 177 species are illustrated and discussed. There are, however, 204 illustrations because of the necessity to show both males and females of some species, especially the wrasses and parrotfishes, which exhibit marked differences in color with sex. For a few, the diverse juvenile form is figured as well.

Approximately 680 species of fishes are known from the Hawaiian Islands, if some not yet recorded in formal scientific papers are counted (but excluding species introduced by man). If those which are pelagic, inhabit depths greater than 100 fathoms, or live in freshwater are eliminated, about 420 species remain that could be designated reef and inshore fishes.

By adhering strictly to the category "reef fish," the presentation can be restricted to those fishes which actually reside on coral reefs. Omitted therefore are the sand and mud-bottom fishes, such as mullet and threadfin, and the larger roving predaceous forms such as the sharks, jacks, and barracudas, even though they may be seen over reefs and may prey upon reef fishes. Still, there are far more species than can be presented in such a limited work. The decision on which Hawaiian reef fishes to select has been a difficult one. In general, those that are incorporated into the book satisfy the stipulations of being abundant and conspicuous. Some common fishes such as certain scorpionfishes that match their surroundings well are overlooked by most observers and are therefore excluded. So also are many of the small gobies and blennies. On the other hand, some of the strikingly colored species such as certain butterflyfishes are included even though they are not very common.

From the standpoint of biogeography, Hawaii represents a subprovince of the vast tropical Indo-Pacific region which stretches from East Africa to the islands of eastern Oceania. In the species accounts below a distribution given merely as Indo-Pacific means that the fish occurs throughout this region. This does not imply that it has been collected at every island group and along every continental shore in the area, but that it could be expected from any of these localities in the proper habitat. Strictly speaking, the term Indo-Pacific should be stated as Indo-West-Pacific to stress the exclusion of the tropical eastern Pacific region, a faunal zone distinctly different from the central and western Pacific (though there are a few shore fishes that have crossed the broad expanse of open ocean that separates the islands of Oceania from the coast of the Americas and offshore islands). Although most of the fishes (and other forms of marine life) of the Hawaiian Islands are found throughout Oceania, and many range into the Indian Ocean as well, a surprising 30% of the reef and shore fishes are unique to the Hawaiian chain.

Some of these endemic fishes, that is, those restricted to Hawaii, have no close relatives outside the archipelago and may be relics, but most are clearly derivatives of species that occur elsewhere in the Indo-Pacific. The Hawaiian populations have evolved independently due to the great isolation of this island group. Often it is difficult to decide if a Hawaiian variant has differentiated enough to be regarded as a full species or if it should be treated as a subspecies (in which case there would be a third part to the scientific name).

Johnston Island, lying about 750 miles southwest of the Hawaiian chain, is an outlier of the Hawaiian marine biota. When the distribution of a fish is given as Hawaiian Islands, this usually includes Johnston Island as well (though there are a number of Hawaiian fishes not yet recorded from there and some species occur at Johnston that are not found in Hawaii).

It is interesting to note how often the most abundant fish of a genus or family in Hawaii is an endemic species. Examples are the milletseed butterflyfish *(Chaetodon miliaris)* among the Chaetodontidae and the saddle wrasse *(Thalassoma duperrey)* of the Labridae. The success of these fishes probably reflects the longer period of time that they have been evolving within, and hence adapting to, the Hawaiian environment.

The illustrations alone should provide for the identification of most of the species of fishes in this book. Nevertheless, descriptive information is given at the start of each species account to emphasize the principal characteristics by which positive identification may be obtained. This is particularly important if one wishes to identify a preserved specimen that has lost its color or a juvenile or a color variant that does not closely resemble the usual adult form.

It has not been possible to avoid scientific terminology, particularly in the descriptions of the fishes or in listing what they eat. A glossary is provided at the back just before the index for the ichthyological and other scientific words employed in this volume.

The counts of the number of fin rays and scales, and sometimes of the gill rakers (protuberances on the opposite side of each gill arch from the gill filaments), are among the most important diagnostic characters used for the identification of fishes. These counts are presented first in the species accounts. The number of spines is given in Roman numerals and the soft rays in Arabic numerals; thus dorsal rays X,12 would mean that the dorsal fin (fin on the back) has 10 spines (generally strong and sharp-tipped) at the front followed by 12 rays (flexible and often branched). In making counts of the soft rays of the dorsal fin and anal fin (fin in the mid line on the bottom of the fish behind the anus) the last two rays are counted as one if they lie close together and share the same basal element. Counts of the rays of the pectoral fins (fin on each side of the body behind the gill opening) include the short, often rudimentary, upper ray. The scale count given most often for a fish is the number in the lateral line in lengthwise series from the upper end of the gill opening to the caudal fin base. Each lateral-line scale has a small pore leading to a tubular canal beneath the scales. The lateral-line system picks up low frequency vibrations, thus a fish might detect, for example, an approaching predator in turbid water before this danger can be seen.

The various body proportions are also important in fish identification. These are usually expressed in terms of the standard length, which is the straight-line distance from the tip of the snout to the base of the tail (more correctly, the caudal fin), or the head length which is measured from the tip of the snout to the end of the opercular membrane (thin tissue at the back of the gill cover). The most common body proportion is the depth which is the maximum height of the body discounting the fins. A depth of 5 or 6 in the standard length would indicate an elongate fish whereas one of 2 or 3 a rather high-bodied one.

In the description of color markings on fishes, the term bar is used for a vertically oriented band and a stripe for a horizontal (or lengthwise) one.

The length given in the species accounts for the various fishes is the maximum total length in inches (one inch is equivalent to 25.4 millimeters). It is difficult to determine the maximum length for many of the species due to few and sometimes conflicting reports of size in the literature and the paucity of large specimens in fish collections (often small specimens are selected for museums as they fit into smaller jars and take less shelf space).

The Bernice P. Bishop Museum in Honolulu, the author's home institution, has one of the three largest and most diverse collections of Indo-Pacific fishes in the world. Nevertheless the number of specimens of many species is inadequate to fully determine the range of variability of some of the diagnostic characters given in the description. Therefore, a specimen that has one more or one less dorsal ray, for example, than is given in the diagnosis, need not be ruled out as the species under consideration on this basis alone.

Knowledge of the food habits of reef fishes is fundamental to the understanding of the complex interrelationships of the assemblage of animals and plants that comprise the reef community. It is through feeding that fishes have their greatest impact on other reef organisms. Such knowledge is also important in the choice of fishes for an aquarium and for their maintenance. In 1967 the author commenced a long-term study of the food habits of Hawaiian reef fishes by underwater observations and the examination of their stomach contents. The majority of fishes collected for this study were obtained by spearing. The data on feeding which are presented in the species accounts in terms of the number of specimens examined are original and for the most part unpublished. This information is given only in summary form in the present book.

The relative abundance of a species of reef fish is an expression not only of how well it obtains its food (usually in keen competition with other species), but on many other aspects of its biology such as its ability to avoid predation (which often involves a competition for shelter), its resistance to parasites and diseases, how rapidly it grows, its reproductive strategy, the success of its eggs and larvae in the pelagic realm, and its ability to tolerate environmental extremes of temperature, salinity, oxygen content, pH, etc.

Our knowledge of these many facets of the biology of fishes is woefully lacking for the great majority of Hawaiian reef species. Only a few broad studies on the biology and life history of local fishes have been undertaken. This information is briefly noted for these species.

In the headings of the species accounts, the scientific names (in italics) are followed by the author (the individual who named the species) and the date of the description. Parentheses around the author's name signify that he described the fish in a different genus than that in current use.

Most of the Indo-Pacific fishes were given their scientific names in the late 18th and the 19th centuries. Many of the species, particularly the common wide-ranging ones, were named more than once by early naturalists. By the law of priority, the oldest name is the valid name (providing it was binomial, was accompanied by a description, and was published on or after 1758, the date of the 10th edition of Linnaeus' *Systema Naturae,* accepted as the starting point for our biological nomenclature). The subsequent names of the same organisms are called junior synonyms, or simply synonyms. Most of these synonyms have been sorted out some years ago but older names are still being unearthed which will replace names now in use. Indeed, some of the names in this book may in time fall to the law of priority. Recent synonyms, especially if they have been widely used, are given in the species accounts herein.

The captions of the illustrations provide the scientific, American, and Hawaiian names of the fishes. The American common name in bold type is listed first, followed by the scientific name, and when known the Hawaiian name. The Hawaiians did not have names for some of the species, especially those with little or no value as food. In some cases there was a Hawaiian name but we are no longer able to link it to a specific fish. For some groups we are left with only a general name, such as 'ala'ihi for squirrelfishes of the genus *Sargocentron.* There were secondary or qualifying names in use by the ancient Hawaiians, but these were not tied by early naturalists in Hawaii to scientific names. The Hawaiian fishermen of today no longer recall which secondary names go with which species of 'ala'ihi.

In the pronunciation of Hawaiian words it is well to remember that every vowel is sounded. Thus 'ala'ihi, phoenetically, is ah-la-ee-hee. The punctuation mark ' is the glottal stop, a common feature of Polynesian languages. It denotes a brief pause at this point in the pronunciation of a word. At one time in the past there was a consonant where each glottal stop is now shown. The macron over a vowel, as in pūhi, indicates a longer sounding of the vowel than usual.

The first Polynesians to colonize Hawaii were probably Marquesans, judging from the study of fish hooks, adzes, and other artifacts at sites on the island of Hawaii which have been radiocarbon dated at about 750 A.D. Curiously, the Hawaiian fish names bear a closer affinity to Tahitian than Marquesan names. A second wave of migration is believed to have commenced from the Society Islands about 1200 A.D., and evidently this culture at least partially supplanted the Marquesan.

Some of the fish names brought by these early Polynesians were applied to species in Hawaii that are similar to but not the same as fishes of French Polynesia. For example, the name nohu was bestowed upon the large Hawaiian scorpionfish *Scorpaenopsis cacopsis*. In Tahiti the nohu is the dreaded *Synanceia verrucosa* whose dorsal spines are the most venomous in the sea. Hawaii is fortunate in not having this fish in its waters. Still, the other members of the scorpionfish family, particularly the lionfish and turkeyfish, are to be respected for the painful wounds their sharp dorsal spines can inflict.

The American common names of Hawaiian fishes are not completely stabilized; often more than one name is locally used for the same species. The choice among conflicting common names for the present book has been based on several considerations besides nomenclatorial popularity. One is to favor an English equivalent to the scientific name; thus *Gymnothorax flavimarginatus* is the yellowmargin moray. Another is to avoid duplication of a common name well established in a different area. Still another is to accept a less ponderous name. For example the one American species of *Canthigaster* (in Florida and the Caribbean) is called the sharpnose puffer. The shorter name toby, used in other English-speaking countries such as Australia and South Africa, is here adopted for the Hawaiian species of this puffer genus.

The end of each caption gives the total length of the fish that was photographed in inches followed in parentheses by the equivalent in millimeters (mm).

ACKNOWLEDGMENTS

The author acknowledges with gratitude the grants from the Juliette M. Atherton Trust and Samuel N. and Mary Castle Foundation in Honolulu for partial support in the preparation of this book. Thanks are due the following persons who have assisted in collecting and curating, providing advice on nomenclature, and supplying information on the habitat and habits of our colorful reef fishes: Gerald R. Allen, Robin W. Bruce, Bruce A. Carlson, Thomas A. Clarke, Charles E. Dawson, William N. Eschmeyer, William A. Gosline, Phillip C. Heemstra, Douglass F. Hoese, E. Alison Kay, Hari Kojima, Jeffrey M. Leis, Anthony Nahacky, Helen A. Randall, Gail Roper, William F. Smith-Vaniz, Victor G. Springer, Paul Struhsaker, Arnold Y. Suzumoto, A. Bradley Tarr, Leighton R. Taylor, Spencer W. Tinker, Gordon W. Tribble, Robin S. Waples, Jeffrey T. Williams, Eleanor H. Williamson, and Lester Zukeran. Also helpful have been the staff of the Aquatic Resources Division of the Department of Land and Natural Resources of the State of Hawaii, the Honolulu Laboratory of the National Marine Fisheries Service, and the Tamashiro Market.

CLASSIFICATION

LIZARDFISHES (SYNODONTIDAE)

The lizardfishes have a reptile-like head with a large mouth and numerous slender sharp teeth; the tongue has inward-pointing teeth; the body is elongate and round in cross-section; the fins are without spines; an adipose fin (a small fleshy fin on the back between the dorsal and caudal fin) is present. There is a single high dorsal fin of 10 to 14 rays; the pelvic fins have 8 or 9 rays. Most species have a series of irregular dark blotches along the side. These fishes are most often seen on sedimentary bottoms into which they can nearly completely bury themselves. Typically they feed by swift upward movement from the bottom; their prey consists mainly of small fishes. They are not good aquarium fishes because of their strong predilection to feed on live fishes. They are readily caught by hook and line; when the water is shallow they are sometimes taken while trolling. The late larval stage, which may reach more than 2 inches in length in some species, is slender, transparent, with a row of prominent internal black spots ventrally on the body. Nine species are known from Hawaiian waters. The three discussed below are often observed in and around reefs, though they also occur in other habitats. Lizardfishes are not highly esteemed as food.

1. *Synodus variegatus* (Lacepède), 1803. **variegated lizardfish, 'ulae**
Dorsal rays 11 to 13; anal rays 8 to 10; lateral-line scales 57 to 62; rows of scales between lateral line and dorsal fin 5 or 6; one row of teeth showing at edge of lips; membranous flap on hind edge of anterior nostril narrow and pointed. A common species, widespread in the Indo-Pacific region. Attains about 10 inches. *S. ulae* Schultz is a closely related species from Hawaii and Japan, also of large size, which differs in having 62 to 68 lateral-line scales, 13 or 14 dorsal rays, and a spatulate nasal flap.

2. *Synodus binotatus* Schultz, 1953. **twospot lizardfish, 'ulae**
Dorsal rays 12 to 14; anal rays 8 to 10; lateral-line scales 52 to 56; rows of scales between lateral line and dorsal fin 3½; one row of teeth showing at edge of lips; membranous flap on anterior nostril spatulate. Dorsal tip of snout with a pair of small black spots; adipose fin with two blackish cross bands, the basal one darkest. In addition to a lateral series of dark blotches, preserved specimens display longitudinal dark lines on the back. Attains at least 7 inches. Indo-Pacific, in relatively shallow water (generally less than 50 feet).

3. *Saurida flamma* Waples 1982. **orangemouth lizardfish, 'ulae**
Dorsal rays 11; anal rays 9 or 10; pectoral rays 13 to 15; lateral-line scales 53 or 54; rows of scales between lateral line and dorsal fin 3½; vertebrae 52 or 53; three or more rows of small teeth exposed on side of jaws when mouth is closed; palatine teeth (laterally on roof of mouth) in two bands on each side—a narrow elongate outer band and a short broader inner patch (only a single band of palatine teeth on *Synodus*); pectoral fins reach a vertical at the first to third predorsal scales; dorsal fin origin midway between tip of snout and origin of adipose fin; body with a series of indistinct orangish brown bars on mid to lower side; all fins with cross bands (pigment concentrated on rays); region of mouth mottled orange. Attains more than a foot in length. This lizardfish has only

recently been separated from *Saurida gracilis* (Quoy and Gaimard), a shallow-water species of mud or silty sand bottoms which may be found in brackish water. *S. gracilis* differs in usually having 13 pectoral rays, 50 to 52 lateral-line scales, 49 to 51 vertebrae, the pectoral fin tips reaching to fifth or sixth predorsal scales, and the origin of the dorsal fin closer to the adipose fin than the front of the snout.

CONGER EELS (CONGRIDAE)

The Congridae is one of 23 families of eels of the order Anguilliformes (older name Apodes). All true eels share the following characteristics: elongate body, numerous vertebrae, no spines in fins, no pelvic fins, no distinct caudal fin (median fins continuous around tip of tail, except for some of the snake eels), scales reduced or absent, gill opening small, and a leptocephalus larval stage (transparent, long and ribbon-like, with a small head). Congers tend to have rounded bodies anteriorly, becoming laterally compressed posteriorly; they have strong jaws and stout teeth (not long and needle-like as in most morays); the lips have free margins; the posterior nostril is near the eye (not labial); the lateral line is well developed. The family is divisable into two subfamilies: the Heterocongrinae (garden eels), represented by one recently described *Gorgasia* from Hawaii, which are attenuate burrowing species with pectoral fins reduced or absent, restricted gill opening, a short snout, and an oblique mouth with projecting lower jaw; and the Congrinae which have well developed pectoral fins, a relatively large gill opening on lower side, a longer snout, and a near-horizontal mouth. The largest and best known genus of the latter subfamily is *Conger,* of which there are two species in Hawaiian waters. These eels are often locally called white eels and are important as food fishes.

4. *Conger cinereus* Rüppell, 1830.   **mustache conger, pūhi-ūhā**

Origin of dorsal fin over approximate mid-length of pectoral fins; pectoral rays 17 to 20; lateral-line pores anterior to vertical at anus 39 to 42; vertebrae 148 to 152; teeth at edge of jaws compressed, close-set, thus forming a shearing edge. Brownish gray with prominent black margins on median fins, a blackish streak below eye parallel to upper lip (this mark absent in juveniles less than about 8 inches in length) and often with a large blackish area on pectoral fins. *C. cinereus* is known throughout the Indo-Pacific region. In the Hawaiian Islands it differs in having higher meristic data (counts given above for Hawaiian specimens; outside Hawaii there are 15 to 19 pectoral rays, 37 to 41 anterior lateral-line pores, and 139 to 146 vertebrae). The Hawaiian population is regarded as a subspecies, *C. cinereus marginatus* Valenciennes. *Conger oligoporus* Kanazawa, a Hawaiian endemic species, differs from *cinereus* in having the origin of the dorsal fin slightly posterior to a vertical at pectoral fin tips, 35 or 36 lateral-line pores anterior to anus, 15 or 16 pectoral rays, and 137 to 139 vertebrae. *C. cinereus* hides in the reef by day and forages for food at night at which time it characteristically displays alternating dark and light bars on the body. The stomachs of 20 specimens were opened. Nine were empty; ten contained the digested remains of fishes, including the surgeonfish *Acanthurus triostegus* and a filefish (*Cantherhines* sp.) (two eels had also eaten a shrimp and one a crab); one contained only a shrimp. Largest specimen from Hawaii examined, 45 inches.

MORAYS (MURAENIDAE)

Moray eels, known in Hawaii by the general Polynesian name pūhi, are characterized by elongate, muscular, somewhat compressed bodies, narrow jaws, and impressive dentition; there are no pectoral fins; the dorsal and anal fins are confluent with the caudal fin. The largest muraenid genus is *Gymnothorax* (some authors use the generic name *Lycodontis* for the majority of morays and restrict *Gymnothorax* to a small group of species with serrate teeth). The large genus *Uropterygius* is unusual in having rudimentary dorsal and anal fins which are confined to the tip of the tail. Another large genus, *Echidna*, and the monotypic *Gymnomuraena* are unique in possessing low nodular teeth, in contrast to the other genera which have elongate needle-sharp canines. Species of *Echidna* appear to feed mainly on crabs and other crustaceans while the sharp-tooth morays are better adapted to prey upon fishes, though crustaceans and octopuses are often eaten. Morays do not often leave the shelter of holes or crevices in the reef. Some are known to be nocturnal. Morays are capable of inflicting painful wounds, but the danger attributed to them is greatly overstated. They are not apt to bite unless provoked or unless one is foolish enough to place one's hand in the vicinity of their jaws as the author has done on several occasions (even then the chances of being bitten are not great). More than 35 species of morays are known from Hawaiian waters (several are still waiting for scientific names and formal description) which makes them second only to the wrasses in the number of species in the islands. The large number of muraenid species that have become established in Hawaii may be due to the relatively long life in the plankton of their leptocephalus larvae. Morays are far more abundant on Hawaiian reefs than would be indicated from underwater observation alone (use of the ichthyocide rotenone invariably results in an astounding number of muraenids). Their abundance may be related to the absence of native shallow-water species of the large grouper genera *Epinephelus* and *Cephalopholis,* the snapper genus *Lutjanus,* and the emperor genus *Lethrinus.* These carnivorous fishes are well represented at other Indo-Pacific localities where they are major competitors for food with moray eels. In general, morays are more slender when young and stouter-bodied as they grow longer, which accounts in part for the variation of the relationship of body depth to total length given in the species discussions below.

5. ***Gymnothorax meleagris*** **(Shaw and Nodder), 1795.**
whitemouth moray, pūhi-'ōni'o
Depth of body 10 to 15 in length; snout to anus 2.2 to 2.5 in length; front of upper jaw with three inner rows of long fang-like teeth in addition to outer row; teeth on side of jaw in two rows. Brown or yellowish brown with numerous dark-edged white spots; tip of tail with an irregular white blotch; gill opening in a black blotch; inside of mouth white. Attains about 3½ feet. Found throughout most of the tropical Indo-Pacific. Has been confused with two other white-spotted eels in Hawaii, *Gymnothorax nudivomer* (Günther) [*G. xanthostomus* (Snyder) is a synonym] on which the spots are much larger on the tail than elsewhere, and the inside of the mouth is yellow, and *G. nuttingi* (Snyder) which is a deep-water species on which the spots are irregular, more dense, and not dark-edged. The stomachs of 25 *G. meleagris* were opened; seven contained fishes, one a portunid crab, and the rest were empty.

6. ***Gymnothorax flavimarginatus*** **(Rüppell), 1830.** **yellowmargin moray, pūhi-paka**
Depth of body 11 to 18 in length; snout to anus 2.1 to 2.3 in length; large fang-like teeth at front of upper jaw in one median row in addition to outer row; teeth on side of jaw in one row. Mottled dark brown, with a yellow-green margin on fins; gill opening in a black

blotch. Attains at least 4 feet. Widespread in the Indo-Pacific from the Red Sea and East Africa to the Hawaiian Islands and French Polynesia. One of the most common of the larger morays in Hawaii. A bold species, it often makes an appearance when a reef fish has been speared. The stomachs of 24 specimens were opened. Only seven fish contained food; four of these had eaten fishes, one of which was the goatfish *Mulloides flavolineatus,* and the others contained crustacean remains (two were only a single crab claw).

7. *Gymnothorax eurostus* (Abbott), 1860.   **stout moray, pūhi**
Depth of body 10 to 15 in length; snout to anus 2.1 to 2.4 in length; front of upper jaw with three inner rows of long fang-like teeth in addition to outer row; teeth on side of jaw biserial. One of the most variably colored of morays, but generally brown, becoming dark brown posteriorly, with numerous small light yellow spots (more numerous anteriorly); black spots as large or slightly larger than eye more-or-less in rows on about anterior half of body; tip of tail edged in white. Largest specimen examined, 22.5 inches. Anti-tropical in distribution; known in the northern hemisphere from the Hawaiian Islands (where it is the most common inshore moray, though not often seen), Johnston Island (the Indo-Pacific locality of the lowest latitude), Marcus Island, Japan, and Taiwan; in the southern hemisphere it occurs at Easter Island, Pitcairn, Austral Islands, Lord Howe Island, the Capricorn Group of the Great Barrier Reef, and southern Mozambique. Recently it was recorded from Isla del Coco off Costa Rica. The stomachs of 59 Hawaiian specimens were opened. Thirty-seven of these eels were empty, eight had fed on fishes (including an unidentified eel and a wrasse), six on crabs, two on shrimps, one on spiny lobster appendages, and five on unidentified crustaceans.

8. *Gymnothorax undulatus* (Lacepède), 1803.   **undulated moray, pūhi-lau-milo**
Depth of body 10 to 19 in length; snout to anus 2.1 to 2.3 in length; large fang-like teeth at front of upper jaw in a single median row in addition to outer row; teeth on side of jaw uniserial. Irregular large and some small dark brown blotches separated by narrow whitish or yellowish interspaces, thus forming a pattern of interconnected pale lines; upper part of head yellowish. Attains a length of about 3½ feet. Indo-Pacific, varying in abundance with locality; moderately common in Hawaii.

9. *Echidna nebulosa* (Ahl), 1789.   **snowflake moray, pūhi-kāpā**
Body slender, the depth 14 to 20 in length; anus approximately in center of total length, the snout to anus distance 1.9 to 2.1 in length; short stout conical teeth anteriorly in jaws; sides of jaws with small close-set compressed nodular teeth in one or two rows; vomerine teeth nodular, in two rows. White with two rows of large dendritic black blotches containing small yellow spots; numerous small black dots between large blotches which become more numerous and irregularly linear with age. Attains 28 inches. Indo-Pacific. A shallow-water species of rocky bottoms or reef flats. The stomachs of 16 specimens were opened; one contained the vertebral column of a fish, three had crabs, and the rest were empty.

10. *Gymnomuraena zebra* (Shaw), 1797.   **zebra moray, pūhi**
Depth of body 16 to 20 in length; anus much nearer tip of tail than head, the snout to anus distance about 1.5 in total length; dorsal and anal fins restricted to posterior part of tail; numerous molariform teeth (often with a diagonal ridge-like cusp) nearly covering jaws and palate like a cobblestone pavement; about five rows of teeth at front of upper jaw, two rows of smaller teeth on side of upper jaw, five or six rows on vomer, and three rows on lower jaw (at all sites teeth of the median rows much the largest). Chocolate brown with numerous narrow light yellow bars. Reported to attain nearly 5 feet. Indo-Pacific; also recorded from the Tres Marias Islands and the Galapagos Islands in the eastern Pacific. Not common but attracts attention because of its striking color pattern. The stomachs of

five specimens were examined; two were empty, two contained crabs, and the last had crab and pelecypod remains in about equal amounts. Sometimes classified in the genus *Echidna.*

TRUMPETFISHES (AULOSTOMIDAE)

The aulostomid fishes are grouped with the cornetfishes (Fistulariidae), snipefishes (Macrorhamphosidae), shrimpfishes (Centriscidae), ghost pipefishes (Solenostomidae), and pipefishes and seahorses (Syngnathidae) in the order Syngnathiformes. All share the unique feature of a small mouth at the end of a long tubular snout. The trumpetfishes are shallow-water reef fishes with very elongate compressed bodies, VIII to XII slender isolated dorsal spines, followed by a normal dorsal fin, abdominal pelvic fins with 6 rays (no spine), naked head, small ctenoid scales on body, compressed snout, projecting lower jaw with a barbel on chin, minute teeth, and a rounded to rhomboid caudal fin lacking a median filament. They are sometimes confused with cornetfishes which are also very elongate, but the latter have depressed bodies and a long filament extending posteriorly from the middle of the caudal fin. The family consists of a single genus, *Aulostomus,* and three species, one in the eastern Atlantic, one in the western Atlantic, and one in the Indian and Pacific Oceans.

11. *Aulostomus chinensis* (Linnaeus), 1766.   **trumpetfish, nūnū**
Dorsal rays X to XII-IV,25 or 26; anal rays III,25 to 27; pectoral rays 17; scale rows from upper end of gill opening to caudal base about 265; depth of body 11 to 15 in standard length; width of body 1.7 to 2 in depth. Color variable but often orangish brown, usually with longitudinal pale banding, white spots in vertical rows posteriorly on body, two black spots, one above the other in caudal fin, a black spot at each pelvic base, and a black streak on maxilla. A yellow color phase is not uncommon. Widespread in the Indo-Pacific region (though absent from the Red Sea and Persian Gulf); also recorded from islands of the eastern Pacific. Occurs from shallow water to at least 370 feet. Largest Hawaiian specimen collected by author, 27 inches. The stomach contents of 18 specimens consisted mainly of small fishes, including members of the damselfish, surgeonfish, goatfish, cardinalfish, and bigeye families; one fish had eaten a shrimp. Trumpetfish feed by stalking to a close position, then darting forward and sucking in their prey with a lateral expansion of the snout. They sometimes swim with schooling herbivorous fishes, notably the surgeonfish *Acanthurus triostegus,* apparently to take advantage of small fishes being disrupted by the presence of so many fishes grazing on benthic algae in their area. Also trumpetfishes are not infrequently seen swimming in close association with large fishes, particularly parrotfishes, which are also algal feeders; this probably enables them to approach their prey more closely by hiding to one side of these harmless herbivores. Fishes have been found in the stomachs of trumpetfish that seem too large to have passed through their small snouts. One trumpetfish 25 inches in standard length, for example, contained a damselfish (*Stegastes*) 4 inches in standard length and nearly 2 inches deep; yet the depth of the snout was less than 1.2 inches and the width less than 0.3 inches. The membranous tissue forming the floor of the snout, however, is very elastic and capable of great stretching when the snout is expanded to suck in the prey.

PIPEFISHES AND SEAHORSES (SYNGNATHIDAE)

The syngnathid fishes have elongate bodies encased in a series of bony rings, no spines in fins, a single dorsal fin, a tiny anal fin (dorsal and anal fins are rarely absent), and no pelvic fins; the caudal fin is absent on seahorses and a few pipefishes. The tail of seahorses is utilized as a prehensile organ. They are also unique in the vertical orientation of the body with the head directed forward. All of these fishes have slender tubular snouts and tiny mouths. They feed by a rapid pipette-like intake of water with their prey which usually consists of small crustaceans. They are also characterized by peculiar tufted gills, an aglomerular kidney, and a ventral brood pouch on male fish (only a brood patch on some primitive species) in which the young are reared after the eggs are laid and placed there by the female. Two seahorses and six pipefishes are recorded from the Hawaiian Islands, of which the most common is discussed below.

12. *Doryhamphus excisus* Kaup, 1856.   **bluestripe pipefish**
Dorsal rays 23 to 26; pectoral rays 21 to 23; trunk rings 17; tail rings 14 or 15 (usually 14); depth of body 12 to 16 in standard length; snout 2.1 to 2.3 in head; ridges on head and body strongly serrate; brood pouch abdominal. Yellowish gray to orange with a lateral black stripe tinged with red or orange on snout and postorbital head, continuing as a broad dark bluish stripe on upper side of trunk and laterally on tail; broadly expanded caudal fin orange-yellow and red, blotched with blackish, the margins pale. Common and widespread on Indo-Pacific reefs from the shore to at least 75 feet. Also recorded from the Revillagigedo Islands in the eastern Pacific. Largest Bishop Museum specimen, 2.4 inches. A male from Oahu 2.2 inches in standard length was reported with 137 eggs 1.2 mm in average diameter in its brood pouch. This pipefish is usually known in the literature as *D. melanopleura* (Bleeker); however, *D. excisus* is the earliest valid name.

FROGFISHES (ANTENNARIIDAE)

The frogfishes are a very peculiar group of sedentary fishes. Not long ago they were regarded as among our most advanced fishes, hence frequently placed last in fish books which are arranged phylogenetically. Now we believe them to be an offshoot of primitive teleost stock. There are nine species in Hawaii; none are common. Some vary greatly in color, apparently to match the color of the bottom on which they reside. Their resemblance to their surroundings may be enhanced by fleshy protuberances or filaments on the skin. Furthermore, they move very infrequently. It is not surprising that they are often overlooked, even by keen observers. Their shape is rather amorphous, but distinctly compressed. The pectoral fins are limb-like with an "elbow" joint. The small round gill opening is usually found on the basal part of or just posterior to this appendage. The mouth is highly oblique and capacious. The first dorsal spine is modified as a unique fishing pole on the top of the snout. At the tip is a lure which often resembles some normal food item for small fishes. When this is enticingly wiggled, fishes may be attracted to it. Instead of obtaining a meal, however, they may become one. Frogfishes are voracious and therefore not good aquarium fishes if one values the other fishes in the same tank.

13. *Antennarius commersonii* (Shaw), 1804.   **Commerson's frogfish**
Dorsal rays 13; anal rays 8; pectoral rays 11; first dorsal spine (the "fishing pole") about as long as third spine; more than half of the last anal ray joined by a membrane to caudal peduncle. The color can be yellow, red, brown or black or combinations thereof. Largest Bishop Museum specimen, 12 inches. East Indies to Oceania. *A. moluccensis* Bleeker is a junior synonym. *A. pictus* (Shaw) also reaches large size; it differs in having 10 pectoral rays and the last anal ray connected to the peduncle only basally.

SQUIRRELFISHES (HOLOCENTRIDAE)

The squirrelfishes are very spiny reef fishes with large eyes; most are red. The pelvic fins are

I, 7, and there are XI dorsal spines and IV anal spines. The caudal fin is forked. The mouth is moderately large, but the teeth are small. These fishes tend to hide in caves and beneath ledges by day but actively forage for food at night. They feed mainly on crustaceans. Sixteen species occur in Hawaii in the genera *Neoniphon* (a senior synonym of *Flammeo*), *Sargocentron* (a senior synonym of *Adioryx*), *Plectrypops*, *Ostichthys*, *Pristilepis* and *Myripristis*. The formerly large genus *Holocentrus* is now restricted to two Atlantic species. Indo-Pacific squirrelfishes once grouped in *Holocentrus* are presently classified in *Sargocentron* and *Neoniphon*. The fishes of these two genera have a strong spine at the corner of the preopercle; on at least some, this spine is venomous. *S. spiniferum*, the largest species of the family (to about 18 inches), is rare in Hawaii; it is deep-bodied with a solid red spinous dorsal fin. Records of *S. microstoma* from the Hawaiian Islands appear to be in error. The general Hawaiian name for the species of *Sargocentron* and *Neoniphon* is 'ala'ihi. There were secondary Hawaiian names for these fishes (equivalent to the second half of scientific names) but it is no longer certain which of these names apply to various species. The species of *Myripristis*, of which there are four in Hawaii, are popularly known as soldierfishes. The Hawaiian name for these fishes is 'ū'ū, but the Japanese name menpachi has largely replaced it. The larger *Myripristis* in Hawaii are esteemed as food fishes.

14. *Neoniphon sammara* (Forsskål), 1775. **spotfin squirrelfish, 'ala'ihi**
Dorsal rays XI, 12; anal rays IV,8; last dorsal spine longer than penultimate spine and closely adhered to first ray of fin (in contrast to species of *Sargocentron* and *Myripristis* where last dorsal spine is longest and well spaced from first ray); body relatively elongate, the depth about 3.5 in standard length; lower jaw strongly projecting. Silvery with longitudinal rows of maroon spots; a large black spot on dorsal fin between first and fourth spines. Reaches about 10 inches. Ranges from the Red Sea to eastern Oceania. Stomachs of 39 specimens contained small crabs (66.5% by volume), post-larval fishes (15%), other crustaceans and polychaete worms. These food organisms were mainly the larger animals of the zooplankton. The only other Hawaiian member of the genus is *N. aurolineatus* (Liénard) (formerly *scythrops*) which is red with yellow stripes, has 13 or 14 dorsal soft rays, 9 anal soft rays, and is generally found in depths greater than 100 feet.

15. *Sargocentron punctatissimum* (Cuvier and Valenciennes), 1830.
peppered squirrelfish, 'ala'ihi
Dorsal rays XI,12 or 13; anal rays IV,9; pectoral rays 15; depth 2.8 to 2.9 in standard length; two opercular spines about equal. Silvery red, usually with a stippling of dusky pigment; spinous dorsal fin with a row of white spots half way out in fin. To 5 inches. Indo-Pacific. Submarine observations to 600 feet, but most abundant in less than 6 feet. Stomachs of ten specimens taken in early morning hours contained almost entirely small crustaceans, mainly crabs. *S. lacteoguttatum* (Cuvier) is a synonym.

16. *Sargocentron diadema* (Lacepède), 1802. **crown squirrelfish, 'ala'ihi**
Dorsal rays XI,13 or 14; anal rays IV,9; pectoral rays 14; depth about 2.9 in standard length; upper opercular spine the largest. Silvery white and red striped, the red stripes more than twice as broad as the white; spinous dorsal fin deep red, almost black on some individuals, with a white band near base in front part of fin and a broken white band higher in posterior part of fin. Reaches 6.5 inches. Indo-Pacific.

17. *Sargocentron xantherythrum* (Jordan and Evermann), 1903.
Hawaiian squirrelfish, 'ala'ihi
Dorsal rays XI,13; anal rays IV,10; pectoral rays 15; depth 3.0 to 3.1 in standard length; upper of two opercular spines much larger. Silvery white and red-striped without dusky

pigmentation; spinous dorsal fin entirely red except membranes at spine tips which are white. To 6.5 inches. Known only from the Hawaiian Islands. The most common squirrelfish at depths of about 60 feet.

18. *Sargocentron tiere* **(Cuvier and Valenciennes), 1829.**

Tahitian squirrelfish, 'ala'ihi

Dorsal rays XI,14; anal rays IV,9; pectoral rays 15; lateral-line scales 47 to 51; depth of body 2.7 to 2.8 in standard length; upper opercular spine slightly longer than lower; mouth relatively large, the maxilla reaching a vertical at hind edge of pupil. Deep red with faint blue iridescent stripes along centers of scales in life; tip of interspinous membranes of dorsal fin white, and a white blotch on each membrane. Largest specimen collected by author, 11.5 inches. Indo-Pacific. Not common in Hawaii. Type locality, Tahiti; the scientific name is from the Tahitian name tiere for this species. *S. tiere* occurs in as little as 10 feet; however there are submarine observations to 600 feet.

19. *Myripristis berndti* **Jordan and Evermann, 1903.   bigscale soldierfish, 'u'u**
Dorsal rays X-I,13 to 15 (usually 14); anal rays IV,11 to 13 (usually 12); lateral-line scales 28 to 31 (usually 29); small scales on lower half of pectoral axil (absent on the other Hawaiian species of the genus); lower jaw of adults strongly projecting when mouth is closed; interorbital space narrow, 4.3 to 5.2 in head. Red; dark edge of opercular membrane extending slightly below opercular spine; outer part of spinous dorsal fin orange-yellow. Reaches 11 inches. This species has the broadest distribution of the genus — islands of the tropical eastern Pacific to East Africa. The most common species in Hawaii from depths of about 50 to at least 150 feet. *M. chryseres* Jordan and Evermann ranges even deeper; it is distinctive in having yellow on the fins and 32 to 38 lateral-line scales. *M. berndti* is often misidentified as *M. murdjan* (Forsskål).

20. *Myripristis amaena* **(Castelnau), 1873.   brick soldierfish, 'u'u**
Dorsal rays X-I,13 to 16 (usually 15); anal rays IV,12 to 15 (usually 13); lateral-line scales 32 to 36 (modally 34); lower jaw not projecting when mouth is closed; interorbital width 3.0-4.0 in head. Red; dark pigment on opercular membrane extending slightly below opercular spine; outer part of spinous dorsal fin red. Largest Bishop Museum specimen, 10.3 inches, from Johnston Island. Known only from islands of Oceania. The most common Hawaiian species of the genus in about 30 feet or less. *M. argyromus* Jordan and Evermann is reported as a synonym.

21. *Myripristis kuntee* **Cuvier and Valenciennes, 1831.**

shoulderbar soldierfish, 'u'u

Dorsal rays X-I,15 to 17; anal rays IV,14 to 16; lateral-line scales 37 to 44 (modally 40); lower jaw of adults slightly projecting when mouth is closed; interorbital width 3.6 to 4.4 in head. Red; a broad dark reddish-brown bar from upper end of gill opening to pectoral axil; outer part of spinous dorsal fin yellow. A small species; the largest specimen measures 7.6 inches. Indo-Pacific. *M. borbonicus* Cuvier and Valenciennes and *M. multiradiatus* Günther are synonyms.

SCORPIONFISHES (SCORPAENIDAE)

The scorpionfishes are named for the venomous spines which are possessed by many of the species. Other characteristics include the suborbital stay (a bony reinforcing plate which runs from the second suborbital bone across the cheek to the preopercle), various ridges and spines on the head, a large mouth, and small villiform teeth. Often there are fleshy flaps and cirri on the head and body which, along with the variable mottled color pattern, enable these fishes to match their surroundings closely. Scorpionfishes are sedentary and move infrequently. They feed mainly on crustaceans and fishes which make the mistake of venturing near these masters of camouflage. Twenty-five species of scorpionfishes occur in the Hawaiian Islands, of which eight are deep-water forms. Fortunately the infamous stonefish (*Synanceia*), the most venomous of fishes, does not range to Hawaii. The Polynesian name for the stonefish, nohu, has been applied by the Hawaiians to the two larger species of *Scorpaenopsis*. However, Hawaii does have a *Pterois* and a *Dendrochirus* (*Brachirus* is a synonym) which are capable of inflicting extremely painful wounds with their spines.

22. *Sebastapistes coniorta* Jenkins, 1903.　　　speckled scorpionfish
Dorsal rays XII,9 (rarely 10); anal rays III,5; pectoral rays 15 to 17 (usually 16); scales ctenoid; vertical scale rows between upper end of gill opening and caudal fin base 50 to 55; no coronal spines (a pair of spines on each side of mid-dorsal line in hind part of interorbital space); no occipital pit; palatine teeth present. Speckled with numerous small dark brown spots; no large black spot on dorsal fin. Largest specimen, 3.8 inches. Common on reefs from near shore to at least 80 feet in the Hawaiian Islands and Johnston Island; more study is needed to determine if a similar form elsewhere in the Indo-Pacific is the same species. Usually found hiding among branches of coral. Feeds mainly on crabs and shrimps. Sometimes classified in the genus *Scorpaena*.

23. *Sebastapistes ballieui* (Sauvage), 1875.　　　spotfin scorpionfish
Dorsal rays XII,9; anal rays III,5; pectoral rays 16; scales cteniod; vertical scale rows between upper end of gill opening and caudal fin base 40 to 45; coronal spines present (a posteriorly directed spine on each side of mid-dorsal line at the hind part of interorbital space); no occipital pit; palatine teeth present. Body without numerous small dark spots; a large black spot usually present on spinous dorsal fin between spines VII and X. Largest specimen, 4.6 inches. A common shallow-water species definitely known only from the Hawaiian Islands, though a closely related species occurs at other Indo-Pacific locations. *S. corallicola* Jenkins is a synonym. *S. ballieui* has been confused with *S. galactacma* Jenkins, another small Hawaiian scorpionfish, but the latter is readily distinguished by its cycloid scales (smooth-edged, but may be emarginate).

24. *Scorpaenodes parvipinnis* (Garrett), 1864.　　　lowfin scorpionfish
Dorsal rays XIII,9; anal rays III,5; pectoral rays 17 to 19 (usually 18); scales strongly ctenoid; vertical scale rows from upper end of gill opening to caudal fin base 45 to 55; snout and interorbital space scaled; dorsal spines short, usually none exceeding eye diameter in length; suborbital ridge with more than 5 spinous points (usually at least 10 on adults); no occipital pit; palatine teeth absent; body may be covered with small filaments. Color variable but often pale salmon pink with faint irregular dark bars. Largest Bishop Museum specimen, 4.5 inches. A cryptic species not easily seen underwater. Known from coral reefs and rocky bottoms from the Red Sea and east African coast to French Polynesia in the depth range of a few feet to at least 160 feet. One of five species of the genus recorded from Hawaii.

25. *Scorpaenopsis diabolus* Cuvier and Valenciennes, 1829.
devil scorpionfish, nohuʻomakaha
Dorsal rays XII,8 to 10 (usually 9); anal rays III,5 (rarely 6); pectoral rays 18 (rarely 17); scales ctenoid; vertical scale rows between upper end of gill opening and caudal fin base about 45; nape and back beneath spinous portion of dorsal fin highly arched; interorbital width greater than eye diameter; palatine teeth absent; a broad deep depression beneath eye and another termed the occipital pit mid-dorsally behind eyes. Reaches about a foot in length. Indo-Pacific. The only humpbacked species in Hawaii; has been identified

previously as *gibbosa,* but the latter is confined to the Indian Ocean. When alarmed, *diabolus* and its near relatives move their pectorals forward, revealing the largely bright orange and yellow inner surface of the fins — evidently as warning coloration. More apt to be found in the shallows than the following species.

26. *Scorpaenopsis cacopsis* **Jenkins, 1901.**   **titan scorpionfish, nohu**
Dorsal rays XII,9 (rarely 8); anal rays III,5 (rarely 6); pectoral rays 17 to 19 (usually 18); scales ctenoid; vertical scale rows between upper end of gill opening and caudal fin base 50 to 55; interorbital width greater than eye diameter; palatine teeth absent; a broad depression beneath anterior part of eye; shallow occipital pit present; third dorsal spine usually longest; often with fleshy flaps on head and body (particularly conspicuous are tentacles on chin). Mottled orange-red. A large species; attains about 20 inches. Known only from the Hawaiian Islands where it occurs from about 15 to at least 200 feet. In spite of its size, this fish is usually overlooked by divers because of its immobility and remarkable resemblance to its surroundings. Seven of 15 with full stomachs had eaten small fishes, including a squirrelfish, surgeonfish, and trumpetfish. A highly prized food fish. Another shallow-water species of the genus, *S. brevifrons* Eschmeyer and Randall, differs in having a shorter blunter snout and the fourth to sixth dorsal spines the longest.

27. *Taenianotus triacanthus* **Lacepède, 1802.**   **leaf scorpionfish**
Dorsal rays usually XII,10; anal rays III,6 (rarely 5); pectoral rays 14 or 15 (usually 14), all the rays unbranched; scales seemingly absent (but modified as tiny papillae); body deep and very compressed, the width contained about 3 times in the depth; dorsal fin elevated, the longest spines (second and third) contained 1.2 to 1.3 times in head, the origin of the fin slightly posterior to hind edge of eye; last dorsal ray linked by membrane to upper edge of caudal fin. Color varying from light red to yellow, brown, and black, blotched with whitish and dark pigment. Attains a maximum length of about 4 inches. Indo-Pacific; recorded from depths of 2 to 440 feet. Feeds on small crustaceans and fishes; very reluctant to accept anything but live food in an aquarium. Often rocks to and fro to simulate a bit of flotsam such as a leaf being moved by surge; it will even do this in an aquarium. This species periodically sheds the cuticular layer of its skin.

28. *Iracundus signifer* **Jordan and Evermann, 1903.**   **decoy scorpionfish**
Dorsal rays XII,9 (rarely 10); anal rays III,5; pectoral rays 17 or 18 (usually 18); scales ctenoid; vertical scale rows from upper end of gill opening to caudal fin base 65 to 75; palatine teeth absent; fourth dorsal spine notably elongate in specimens greater than about 2 inches in standard length; no spines on suborbital ridge except one at the end in front of preopercle. Mottled red with a small black spot between second and third dorsal spines; base of spinous portion of dorsal fin largely colorless. Largest Bishop Museum specimen, 5.1 inches. Known only from Hawaii until 1965 when the species was recorded from the Cook Islands. In recent years, however, the author has collected it in the Society Islands, southern Tuamotus, Austral Islands, Pitcairn Group, Marquesas, Taiwan and Mauritius. *I. signifer* uses the spinous portion of its dorsal fin as a lure; the fin mimics a small fish, with the black spot as the eye, the elongate fourth dorsal spine as its dorsal fin, and the gap between the first and second spines as the mouth. The transparent lower part of the fin tends to separate the lure from the body of the scorpionfish. When luring, the dorsal fin is snapped from side to side by the anterior spines and a sinuous wave passes each time down the fin giving an amazing resemblance to a small fish in motion.

29. *Dendrochirus barberi* **(Steindachner), 1900.**   **Hawaiian lionfish**
Dorsal rays XIII,8 to 10 (usually 9); anal rays III,5; pectoral rays 17 or 18 (rarely 17); scales ctenoid; vertical scale rows from upper end of gill opening to caudal fin base 50 to 55; pectoral fins large, the longest rays reaching to or beyond rear base of anal fin, the

second to ninth rays branched, the membranes here extending to margin of fin; dorsal spines long, the longest more than half body depth, the membranes deeply incised. Greenish to reddish brown with dark bars; dark cross bands in fins, the pigment in soft portions mainly as spots on the rays. Largest Bishop Museum specimen, 6.5 inches. Known only from the Hawaiian Islands; the author has collected specimens in the range of 3 to 160 feet. *D. hudsoni* Jordan and Evermann and *D. chloreus* Jenkins are synonyms.

30. *Pterois sphex* Jordan and Evermann, 1903.   **Hawaiian turkeyfish**
Dorsal rays XIII,10 (rarely 11); anal rays III,6; pectoral rays 16 (rarely 15); pectoral fin rays long, reaching beyond base of dorsal and anal fins, unbranched, free from membranes for about half their length; dorsal spines very long, the longest about equal to body depth, the membranes deeply incised. Alternating bars of brown and whitish or pink on body, the pale bars containing one or more narrow brownish red bands. Reaches perhaps 9 inches (largest specimen examined, 8.3 inches). Restricted to the Hawaiian Islands, where it is the only member of the genus. Has been collected in the depth range of 10 to 400 feet. By day generally concealed beneath ledges or in caves; feeds at night on crustaceans. Evidently the venom of the spines of this species is not as virulent as other *Pterois,* but still to be respected.

GROUPERS AND SEA BASSES (SERRANIDAE)

The family Serranidae is one of the least specialized of the largest order of fishes, the Perciformes. Thus many of its characteristics, such as thoracic pelvic fins with I spine and 5 rays, anal fin with III spines, caudal fin with 15 or 17 principal rays, opercle with 3 spines, and a single dorsal fin (rare exceptions), ally it with a number of other families of fishes. Still other characters which are singly only a little more diagnostic include a protruding lower jaw, the hind part of the maxilla exposed on the cheek, bands of small teeth (some depressible) in jaws, usually with stout fixed canines at the front, small ctenoid scales, and nearly always a serrate preopercular margin. The groupers and sea basses are bottom-dwelling and carnivorous; they feed mainly on fishes and crustaceans. Most, if not all, are hermaphroditic, generally beginning their mature life as females and changing over later to males. The family has its greatest development in tropical and subtropical seas where it is one of the most important groups of commercial fishes. Hawaii is an exception to this; only 17 naturally occuring species of serranid fishes are found in the islands, of which only two are groupers (both *Epinephelus,* one a rare giant species and the other, *E. quernus* Seale, a deep-water resident). The absence of shallow-water groupers in Hawaii is not fully understood. It is suspected that these fishes have a relatively short larval life and are thus not likely to survive the long distances that they would have to be transported in ocean currents from another shoal warm-water area of the Pacific to Hawaii. Beginning in 1955, several species of groupers were introduced from French Polynesia. Only one, *Cephalopholis argus* Bloch and Schneider has become established; it is dark-colored with small bright blue spots. Most of the Hawaiian Serranidae fall into the subfamily Anthiinae; these are generally small colorful species that feed on zooplankton; the majority occur at depths not normally penetrated by SCUBA divers.

31. *Anthias thompsoni* (Fowler), 1923.   **Hawaiian anthias**
Dorsal rays X,16; anal rays II,7; pectoral rays usually 21; lateral-line scales 50 to 58; depth of body 2.7 to 3.3 in standard length; third to tenth dorsal spines about equal; caudal fin lunate, the lobes filmentous (more so in males); pelvic fins not reaching or barely reaching anus; teeth on vomer in a triangular patch; edge of posterior half of orbit

crenulate; head fully scaled except lips and a narrow zone in front of eye. Light red, the centers of the scales yellow, shading gradually to whitish ventrally; a lavender streak from snout under eye to lower edge of opercle. Males pale lavender ventrally; also they develop lavender on upper and lower edges of the caudal fin. Males are larger than females; largest Bishop Museum specimen, 8.5 inches. Restricted to the Hawaiian Islands. Rare in less than 50 feet, but abundant in deeper areas, particularly at escarpments. Deepest collection, 480 feet. Feeds on zooplankton. Formerly classified in the genus *Caesioperca*. Three other *Anthias* have recently been described from Hawaii; *A. bicolor* Randall which is salmon dorsally and abruptly lavender-pink ventrally, the second and third dorsal spines of the male very prolonged; it has 57 to 64 lateral-line scales and 19 or 20 pectoral rays; and *A. ventralis* Randall which is yellow and lavender with elongate pelvic and anal fins, 40 to 46 lateral-line scales, and 9 anal soft rays; and the deep-water *A. fucinus* Randall and Ralston which has 34-36 lateral-line scales.

FLAGTAILS (KUHLIIDAE)

The flagtails, sometimes called mountain basses, are a small family of fishes consisting only of the genus *Kuhlia* and two Australian freshwater genera. They share many characters with the family Serranidae from which they are most readily distinguished externally by a well developed scaly sheath on the dorsal and anal fins. *Kuhlia* is distinguished from the Australian freshwater genera by having a forked tail and complete lateral line. There is a single continuous dorsal fin, though deeply notched; the mouth is oblique; the eyes are large. On some species the caudal fin is marked with black cross bands or margins, hence the common name flagtails. Those fish residing in freshwater may exhibit different color from individuals of the same species in the sea. Apparently only one native species of *Kuhlia* occurs in the Hawaiian Islands.

32. *Kuhlia sandvicensis* (Steindachner), 1876.   Hawaiian flagtail, āholehole
Dorsal rays X,11 or 12; anal rays III,11; pectoral rays 14 to 16; lateral-line scales 49 or 50; body moderately deep, the depth 2.35 to 2.65 in standard length, and compressed; spinous portion of dorsal fin higher than the soft; two spines on opercle; villiform teeth in bands in jaws. Silvery, with bluish tones on the back. Attains a maximum length of about 1 foot. Known only from the Hawaiian Islands; found in marine, brackish, and freshwater environments. Primarily nocturnal. Adults in the sea feed mainly on planktonic crustaceans but also on polychaete worms, insects and algae. Fish grow to about 4 inches by the end of their first year and 6 or 7 inches by the end of the second. Maturity is attained at a length of 6 to 8 inches. Spawning occurs year-around, but predominately during winter and spring months. An excellent food fish.

BIGEYES (PRIACANTHIDAE)

The bigeyes are well named for their very large eyes. They are also characterized by a relatively deep compressed body, a very oblique mouth, small conical teeth in a narrow band in jaws, a single unnotched dorsal fin with X spines, small ctenoid scales, head including maxilla scaled, and pelvic fins broadly joined to body by a membrane. Usually they are red. Four species occur in the Hawaiian Islands, but only the two discussed below are apt to be encountered in shallow water. Generally, they are easily approached underwater. Fine-eating fishes.

33. *Heteropriacanthus cruentatus* (Lacepède), 1801.   glasseye, 'āweoweo
Dorsal rays X,13; anal rays III,14; pectoral rays 17 to 19 (usually 18); lateral-line scales 60 to 68; scale rows between upper end of gill opening and caudal fin 94 to 113; a flat spine at corner of preopercle extending to edge of operculum; border of preopercle broadly scaleless; pelvic fins not long, their length contained 1.5 to 1.7 times in length of head; caudal fin truncate, slightly rounded, or slightly double emarginate. Color variable, from silvery pink through mottled red to solid red; faint dark dots in median fins, especially the caudal. Attains about 1 foot. Circumtropical. Feeds mainly on the larger animals of the zooplankton, such as larval fishes, crab and other crustacean larvae, polychaetes, and cephalopods. Generally found in caves by day.

34. *Priacanthus meeki* Jenkins, 1903.   Hawaiian bigeye, 'āweoweo
Dorsal rays X,13 to 15 (usually 14); anal rays III,14 or 15 (usually 15); pectoral rays 19 or 20; lateral-line scales 74 to 82; scale rows between upper end of gill opening and caudal base 114 to 141; no prominent spine at corner of preopercle on adults; no broad scaleless region at border of preopercle; pelvic fins moderately long, their length contained 1.0 to 1.3 times in head; caudal fin emarginate. Red with a row of small indistinct brownish red blotches along lateral line. Attains at least 12 inches in length. Apparently confined to the Hawaiian Islands. Closely related to *P. hamrur* (Forsskål).

CARDINALFISHES (APOGONIDAE)

The cardinalfishes are named for the red color of many of the species. They have two dorsal fins, the first of VI to VIII spines (first spine often very small), II anal spines, large eyes, a moderately large oblique mouth, and a double-edged preopercle. They are small, carnivorous, and usually nocturnal. By day they tend to hide in caves or crevices in the reefs, sometimes in aggregations; at night they feed individually, primarily on the zooplankton. Males incubate the eggs in the mouth (not yet reported for two small subfamilies). Nine species are recorded from the Hawaiian Islands; two others remain to be described. The Hawaiian name for all these fishes is 'upāpalu.

35. *Apogon kallopterus* Bleeker, 1856.   iridescent cardinalfish, 'upāpalu
Dorsal rays VII-I,9; anal rays II,8; pectoral rays 13 or 14; lateral-line scales 24 or 25; gill rakers 17 to 19; palatine teeth present; both borders of preopercle strongly serrate; caudal fin forked. Light brown with blue-green and yellow iridescence; a narrow dark brown stripe from snout to eye, continuing more broadly and diffusely behind eye along side of body (nearly absent on large individuals), and ending in a dark spot at caudal base centered just above lateral line; a dark streak at front of first dorsal fin, basally in second dorsal and anal fins, on second pelvic ray, and along upper and lower edges of caudal fin. Attains about 6 inches. Indo-Pacific; often the most common shallow-water cardinalfish where it occurs. *A. snyderi* Jordan and Evermann is a synonym.

36. *Apogon taeniopterus* Bennett, 1835.   bandfin cardinalfish, 'upāpalu
Dorsal rays VII-I,9; anal rays II,8; pectoral rays 13; lateral-line scales 25; gill rakers 21 to 24; palatine teeth present; both borders of preopercle strongly serrate; caudal fin forked. Color pale with iridescent hues, the edges of the scales brown (especially dorsally), some specimens with dark spots on lower side; a narrow dark stripe on snout; a little dusky pigment behind eye; a prominent black band, edged in white, at front of first dorsal fin, basally in second dorsal and anal fins, near lateral edge of pelvic fins and near upper and lower edges of caudal fin; a wedge-shaped blackish bar near middle of caudal fin linking

black bands in lobes of fin (less pigment on bar near center of fin of some specimens). Reaches a length of 7 inches. A common species in Hawaii but few records elsewhere; the author has collected it in Mauritius, Tahiti, Pitcairn, and the Marshall Islands. *A. menesemus* Jenkins and *A. menesemops* Lachner are synonyms.

37. *Apogon maculiferus* **Garrett, 1863.**   spotted cardinalfish, 'upāpalu
Dorsal rays VII-I,9; anal rays II,8; pectoral rays 13 or 14 (usually 14); lateral-line scales 25; gill rakers 20 or 21; palatine teeth present; outer border of preopercle serrate, inner border nearly smooth (usually a few small spinules near angle); caudal fin forked. Pale pinkish with iridescence; dark yellowish brown spots in longitudinal rows along scale centers. Reaches a length of 5½ inches. Restricted to the Hawaiian chain. Collections have ranged in depth from 3 to 95 feet.

38. *Apogonichthys perdix* **Bleeker, 1854.**   Waikiki cardinalfish, 'upāpalu
Dorsal rays VII-I,9; anal rays II,8; pectoral rays 14; lateral-line scales 23; gill rakers 13 to 15; palatine teeth absent; preopercular margins smooth; caudal fin rounded. Light reddish brown with indistinct small brown blotches and white flecks; faint brown streaks radiating from posterior edge of eye, the most conspicuous across upper end of opercle; caudal fin brownish red with a whitish margin and brown submarginal band. Largest Bishop Museum specimen, 2.3 inches. Indo-Pacific but known from relatively few localities; a shallow-water species. *Apogonichthys waikiki* Jordan and Evermann is a synonym.

39. *Foa brachygramma* **(Jenkins), 1903.**   bay cardinalfish, 'upāpalu
Dorsal rays VII-I,9; anal rays II,8; pectoral rays 12; lateral line interrupted, the anterior portion with 10 to 12 pored scales, ending beneath second dorsal fin; gill rakers 14 to 16; palatine teeth present; both margins of preopercle smooth; caudal fin rounded; deepest bodied of Hawaiian cardinalfishes, the depth 2.2 to 2.5 in standard length. Yellowish brown with golden reflections. Largest Bishop Museum specimen, 3.1 inches. Abundant around dead coral, sponges, and pilings in shallow bays and harbors, but also known from deeper water; one haul off Molokai containing this species was made in 43 to 73 fathoms. Recorded from East Africa, the Philippines and the Hawaiian Islands.

MORWONGS (CHEILODACTYLIDAE)

The morwongs are a small family of moderate-sized benthic fishes which occur in temperate and subtropical waters. The largest number of species are found in Australia. In the northern hemisphere there are but four species, three of which occur in China and Japan, and one in the Hawaiian Islands. These fishes are distinctive in the large number of dorsal spines and rays (XIV to XXII spines and 21 to 39 soft rays), forked caudal fin, thick lips, small mouth, and small teeth (none on roof of mouth). The lower pectoral rays are unbranched, thickened, and partially separated from the fin membranes (the same pectoral ray structure is found in the following family, the hawkfishes).

40. *Cheilodactylus vittatus* **Garrett, 1864.**   Hawaiian morwong
Dorsal rays XVI or XVII, 29 to 34; anal rays III,8; pectoral rays 14 (upper two and lower six unbranched, the lower rays thickened, some elongate); lateral-line scales 59 to 65; dorsal profile of head above eye markedly convex; body moderately deep, the depth 2.5 to 2.6 in standard length, and somewhat compressed, the width 2.5 to 3.2 in depth; fourth dorsal spine notably the longest, 1.0 to 1.3 in head; adults with a pair of bony protuberances on forehead in front of eyes and a second pair at front of snout. Light olivaceous with two

diagonal black bands on body and three on head, one of which passes from nape to axil of pectoral fin; edge of gill opening and region around lips orange-red. Attains a maximum length of about 16 inches. Formerly believed to be restricted to the Hawaiian Islands, but now known to occur also in the Southern Hemisphere at New Caledonia and Lord Howe Island. Relatively rare in Hawaii; usually not seen in less than about 60 feet. Feeds on a wide variety of small invertebrate animals such as crabs, shrimps and other crustaceans, polychaete worms, mollusks, heart urchins, and foraminifera. *Gregoryina gygis* Fowler and Bean is a synonym, based on a prejuvenile taken from a tern's nest. Sometimes classified in the genus *Gonüstius*, now regarded as a subgenus.

HAWKFISHES (CIRRHITIDAE)

The hawkfishes are a tropical family of 35 species which may be distinguished by having pectoral fins of 14 rays, the lower five to seven of which are unbranched and usually enlarged, a single dorsal fin of X spines which is notched between spinous and soft portions, one or more cirri projecting from the tips of the dorsal spines, and a fringe of cirri on the hind edge of the anterior nostril. These fishes usually rest upon the bottom; their thickened pectoral rays may serve to wedge them in cracks in the reef. Six species occur in the Hawaiian area.

41. *Cirrhitus pinnulatus* (Bloch and Schneider), 1801. **stocky hawkfish, po'o-pa'a**
Dorsal rays X,11; lower seven pectoral rays unbranched; lateral-line scales 39 to 43, four rows of scales above lateral-line; scales on cheek much smaller than body scales; tuft of cirri from each dorsal spine tip. Brown dorsally with indistinct large white blotches, shading to whitish ventrally; body and fins with red spots; head with brownish orange markings. Reaches 11 inches. Indo-Pacific. Lives in surge zone on hard substratum. Stomach contents of 12 specimens consisted of crabs (80%), shrimps, fishes, other crustaceans, sea urchins, and brittle stars. Often taken by hook and line by shore fishermen. *C. alternatus* Gill is a synonym.

42. *Paracirrhites forsteri* (Bloch and Schneider), 1801.
blackside hawkfish, hilu pili-ko'a
Dorsal rays X,11; lower seven pectoral rays unbranched; lateral-line scales 45 to 49; five rows of scales above lateral-line; large scales on cheek in 5 or 6 rows; a single cirrus at tip of each dorsal spine; membranes of spinous dorsal fin little incised. Head and anterior body with small dark red spots; a broad black band on upper posterior half of body, ending in mid-caudal fin. Largest specimen, 8.8 inches. Indo-Pacific. Stomachs of 30 adults were opened; nineteen had eaten small fishes, four contained shrimps, and the rest were empty.

43. *Paracirrhites arcatus* (Cuvier and Valenciennes), 1829.
arc-eye hawkfish, pili-ko'a
Counts and morphology as above; a tri-colored "U"-shaped mark of orange, black and light blue extending diagonally upward from posterior part of eye, and three orange bands, narrowly edged in brown on a light blue zone of interopercle; body with longitudinal orange-brown bands following scale rows. Two basic color phases, one lighter with a broad pinkish white stripe in region of lateral line on posterior two-thirds of body, and the other darker without this pale band. To 5.5 inches. Indo-Pacific. Common; occurs over a wide depth range from shallow water to 1000 feet or more. Stomach contents of 15 specimens consisted of shrimps, small fishes, crabs, other crustaceans, and fish eggs, in that order of importance.

44. *Cirrhitops fasciatus* (Bennett), 1828.　　　　　　**redbar hawkfish, pili-koʻa**

Dorsal rays X,14; anal rays III,6; lower six pectoral rays unbranched; lateral-line scales 48 to 53; four rows of scales above lateral line; scales on cheek large; a tuft of cirri from tip of each dorsal spine; spinous dorsal membranes moderately incised. Red bars on body (broader dorsally, the last on caudal peduncle the darkest), and lesser bars or elongate spots in pale interspaces ventrally; a black spot on opercle. Probably does not exceed 5 inches. Distribution discontinuous: Hawaii, Japan, Madagascar, and Mauritius. Stomach contents of 18 (four empty) indicate about equal feeding on small fishes, shrimps, and crabs, with lesser intake of sipunculids and zooplankton (larval shrimps, copepods, amphipods and larval gastropods).

45. *Amblycirrhitus bimacula* (Jenkins), 1903.　　　　　**twospot hawkfish pili-koʻa**

Dorsal rays X,12; lower five pectoral rays unbranched; lateral-line scales 40 to 42; three rows of scales above lateral line; large scales on cheek in 4 or 5 rows; a tuft of cirri from each dorsal spine tip; membranes of spinous dorsal fin moderately incised. Vertically elongate red spots on body; a prominent black spot on opercle and a larger one below rear base of dorsal fin. Largest specimen, 3.3 inches. Indo-Pacific.

46. *Oxycirrhites typus* Bleeker, 1857.　　　　　　　　**longnose hawkfish**

Dorsal rays X,13; anal rays III,7; lower five or six pectoral rays unbranched; lateral-line scales 51 to 53; four rows of scales above lateral line; two to four cirri from membrane near tip of each dorsal spine; membranes of spinous portion of dorsal fin deeply incised; snout extremely long, its length contained about 2 times in head length. Whitish with horizontal and near-vertical red bands forming a grid pattern; resulting whitish squares with a horizontal row of small red spots, sometimes joined to form red bands. Rarely exceeds 5 inches. The only species of the genus. Known from scattered records from the Red Sea to the Pacific coast of Mexico. Not recorded from Hawaii until 1967. Rare at depths of less than about 100 feet but not uncommon in deeper water. Usually seen perched on black coral or gorgonians. Feeds on small crustaceans and other animals of the plankton as well as a variety of benthic invertebrates. Lays demersal eggs. A popular aquarium fish.

SNAPPERS (LUTJANIDAE)

The snappers are a large family of tropical marine fishes of great commercial importance. Unfortunately, Hawaii possesses but two native shallow-water representatives, though it has nine deeper water species. Recognizing the value of these fishes, the State's Division of Fish and Game attempted to introduce three species of *Lutjanus* to Hawaii from French Polynesia (the first importation from Moorea in 1956) and *Lutjanus guttatus* (Steindachner) from Mexico in 1960. Two of the three *Lutjanus* from French Polynesia have become established (discussed below). The two native shallow-water snappers, *Aphareus furca* (Lacepède) and *Aprion virescens* (Cuvier and Valenciennes), are roving open-water predators that cannot be considered reef fishes though they often prey upon reef-dwelling species. In addition to the general characters of the perciform fishes (see Serranidae), the lutjanid fishes have the maxilla not exposed on the cheek (it slips under the edge of the preorbital when the mouth is closed), no spines on the opercle, the jaws equal (or with the lower slightly projecting), and fixed canine teeth in the jaws; the scales are ctenoid; the caudal fin is emarginate or forked, and the dorsal fin is continuous, with or without a shallow notch between spinous and soft portions; Hawaiian species have X dorsal spines and 10 or 11 soft rays, and the anal fin rays are III,7 to 9.

47. *Lutjanus kasmira* (Forsskål), 1775.   **bluestripe snapper, ta'ape**

Dorsal rays X,15; anal rays III,8; pectoral rays 16; lateral-line scales 47 to 49; depth of body 2.9 to 3.1 in standard length; teeth on vomer in an inverted "V"-shaped patch; a distinct notch in upper preopercular margin. Yellow with four bright blue stripes on upper half of head and body. Largest recorded specimen, 15 inches, but rarely exceeds 10. Indo-Pacific; also recorded from the Galapagos Islands. A common reef species which occurs from shallow water to over 600 feet. Often seen in aggregations by day; appears to be primarily nocturnal. Feeds on crustaceans, especially crabs and shrimps, and small fishes. Introduced from Moorea in 1956, it has become abundant in the Hawaiian Islands. It seems to be increasing its population at the expense of some native fishes more valuable than itself. The Tahitian name ta'ape has been adopted as the Hawaiian name.

48. *Lutjanus fulvus* (Bloch and Schneider), 1801.   **blacktail snapper, to'au**

Dorsal rays X,13 or 14; anal rays III,8; pectoral rays 15 or 16; lateral-line scales 47 or 48; depth of body 2.5 to 2.8 in standard length; teeth on vomer in an inverted "V"-shaped patch; a distinct notch in upper preopercular margin. Gray, the centers of the scales brassy yellow (hence the body appears more yellow than gray); caudal fin blackish with a tinge of red and a narrow white posterior margin; dorsal fin reddish; remaining fins yellow. A record of a specimen 17.5 inches long is probably an error; any length over 13 inches is exceptional. Indo-Pacific. The most common snapper in the Society Islands from whence it was introduced to Hawaii in 1956. Well established in the Hawaiian Islands, where it is known by its Tahitian name to'au, but not yet a common species. The young penetrate inshore water, including brackish environments. Adults feed on crustaceans (54.3% by volume of the stomach contents of 370 specimens collected by the author in the Societies), mainly crabs, and small fishes (42.4%), more at night than during daylight hours. *Lutjanus vaigiensis* (Quoy and Gaimard) is a synonym.

EMPERORS (LETHRINIDAE)

The emperors are an important group of moderate to large-sized perciform fishes which are related to the snappers and grunts and even more closely allied to the porgies (Sparidae). They have a continuous unnotched dorsal fin of X spines and 9 or 10 rays, an anal fin of III spines and 8 to 10 rays, a terminal mouth with moderately thick lips and strong jaws containing stout canine teeth anteriorly and conical to molariform teeth along the sides; there are no teeth on the vomer or palatines; the caudal fin is emarginate to forked. The largest genus is *Lethrinus*, many species of which have elongate snouts. Those with molariform teeth in the jaws tend to feed on mollusks, sea urchins, and other hard-shelled invertebrates. The monotypic *Monotaxis* is the only representative of the family in Hawaiian waters.

49. *Monotaxis grandoculis* (Forsskål), 1775.   **bigeye emperor, mū**

Dorsal rays X,10; anal rays III,9; pectoral rays 14 (rarely 13); lateral-line scales 45 to 47; depth of body 2.2 to 2.9 in standard length (depth increasing with age); eye large, 2.7 to 3.4 in head; snout short, the profile steep; stout canine teeth at front of jaws, and large oval molariform teeth on sides. Silvery, the edges of the scales dark; can rapidly assume a pattern of four broad blackish bars on body. Juveniles pale with four permanent black bars and a more pointed snout than adults. Reported to 2 feet; largest collected by author, 22 inches (7.5 lbs). Indo-Pacific. Known depth range, about 10 to 330 feet. Primarily nocturnal. Gut contents of 48 adults revealed feeding mainly on mollusks (56%), with a significant intake of crabs, sea urchins, heart urchins, and hermit crabs. The hard parts of the prey are crushed by the molars. A wary fish, not easily approached underwater. Excellent eating.

SEA CHUBS (KYPHOSIDAE)

The sea chubs, also known as rudderfishes, are shore fishes of rocky bottoms or coral reefs. They have a relatively deep and moderately compressed body, small head, and a small terminal mouth with incisiform teeth; the maxilla slips partially beneath the preorbital bone when the mouth is closed; the scales are small and ctenoid, covering most of the head and soft portions of the fins; there is a single continuous dorsal fin, and the caudal fin is emarginate to forked. Four species occur in the Hawaiian Islands: three relatively drab *Kyphosus* and the colorful *Sectator ocyurus* (Jordan and Gilbert). *S. ocyurus* is olivaceous yellow dorsally with two bright blue stripes, and white ventrally. It is very rare in Hawaii and may only be a waif from the tropical eastern Pacific. The species of *Kyphosus* have long digestive tracts, and as this would suggest, they feed on plants — usually benthic algae.

50. *Kyphosus bigibbus* Lacepède, 1802.   **brown chub, nenue**
Dorsal rays XI,12 (rarely 11 or 13); anal rays III,11; pectoral rays 18 or 19, lateral-line scales 53 to 59; gill rakers 25 to 27; depth of body 2.2 to 2.5 in standard length; head 3.4 to 3.65 in standard length; teeth incisiform, close-set, in a single row, caudal fin forked; soft portion of dorsal fin not higher than longest dorsal spine. Silvery gray, the edges of the scales dark brown with faint yellowish brown stripes following scale rows; opercular membrane dark brown, almost black. Occasional all-yellow individuals occur, and very rarely, white ones. Mixtures of the gray with yellow or white are evidently crosses of the xanthic and albino forms with normal colored fish. Attains about 2 feet. Indo-Pacific. Feeds on a wide variety of algae from soft filamentous reds such as *Polysiphonia* to coarse browns like *Sargassum* and even *Turbinaria*. A food fish of some value, but not highly regarded in Hawaii. Sometimes misidentified as *K. cinerascens* (Forsskål), a species with an elevated soft portion of the dorsal fin which is rare in Hawaii.

51. *Kyphosus vaigiensis* (Quoy and Gaimard), 1825.   **lowfin chub, nenue**
Dorsal rays XI,14 (rarely 13); and rays III,13; pectoral rays 18 or 19; lateral-line scales 52 to 54; gill rakers 33 to 35; depth of body 2.3 to 2.5 in standard length; teeth incisiform, close-set, in a single row; caudal fin forked; soft portion of dorsal fin not higher than longest dorsal spine. Silver gray with bronze stripes following scale rows; opercular membrane dark orangish brown; two diagonal bronze bands on head, the lowermost passing from upper lip and maxilla nearly to corner of preopercle. Attains about 2 feet. Indo-Pacific. Less common than *K. bigibbus* in Hawaii from which it has only recently been distinguished.

HALFMOONS AND STRIPEYS (SCORPIDIDAE)

This family is considered by many ichthyologists as a subfamily of the Kyphosidae. One major distinction is the the the dentition; the teeth are brush-like in the Scorpididae instead of incisiform and uniserial as in the Kyphosidae. Only a single species is found in Hawaii; it is omnivorous.

52. *Microcanthus strigatus* (Cuvier and Valenciennes), 1831.   **stripey**
Dorsal rays XI,16 or 17; anal rays III,14 or 15 (rarely 15); pectoral rays 15 to 17; lateral-line scales 49 to 52; body deep, the depth 1.75 to 1.9 in standard length; head 2.7 to 3 in standard length; preopercular margin serrate; teeth brush-like; caudal fin emarginate. Yellow with diagonal black stripes. Largest specimen at Bishop Museum, 7.7 inches. Known only from Australia, New Caledonia, China, Japan, and Hawaii. A popular aquarium fish. The young can be caught in tide pools from December to April. Half-inch

fish grow to between 1.5 and 2 inches in four months; at the end of a year they attain about 3 or 4 inches. The young feed on small crustaceans as well as algae. This species will enter brackish areas.

GOATFISHES (MULLIDAE)

The goatfishes, sometimes called surmullets, are easily recognized by the pair of long barbels on the chin which are supplied with chemosensory organs. When searching for food on the bottom, the barbels are held in a forward position and are moved rapidly over the substratum or thrust into the sediment. When not in use they are held medially between the lower part of the gill covers. These fishes are elongate with two widely separated dorsal fins; all Hawaiian species have VIII-9 dorsal rays (first spine very small), and I,7 anal rays; the mouth is small, with the upper jaw slightly protruding; the caudal fin is forked. The species of *Mulloides* (*Mulloidichthys* of most authors) have several irregular rows of tiny teeth in the jaws and 34 to 36 lateral-line scales; the genus *Parupeneus* is characterized by a single row of well-spaced, blunt canine teeth and 27 to 29 lateral-line scales. Not included in the present work are the rare *P. chrysonemus* (Jordan and Evermann), *Upeneus taeniopterus* Cuvier (*U. arge* Jordan and Evermann is a synonym) a fish associated with open stretches of sand or mud bottom, and *Mulloides pflugeri* (Steindachner), a large light red species which usually occurs in relatively deep water. The goatfishes are highly esteemed as food in Hawaii, particularly by oriental people.

53. *Mulloides flavolineatus* (Lacepède), 1801. **yellowstripe goatfish, weke**
Pectoral rays 16 or 17; gill rakers 25 to 30; depth of body 3.6 to 4.7 in standard length; snout 1.7 to 2.6 in head; barbel length 1.4 to 1.8 in head. Silvery white with a yellow stripe on side at level of eye; a black spot usually present on yellow stripe above posterior part of pectoral fin. Reaches about 16 inches. Indo-Pacific. Often occurs in aggregations. The food consists of small crabs, shrimps, fishes, polychaete worms, pelecypods, gastropods, unidentified eggs, hermit crabs, heart urchins, and foraminifera. *M. samoensis* (Günther) is a synonym.

54. *Mulloides vanicolensis* (Cuvier and Valenciennes), 1831.
yellowfin goatfish, weke-'ula
Pectoral rays 16 or 17; gill rakers 32 to 36; depth of body 3.3 to 3.9 in standard length; snout 2.1 to 2.6 in head; barbel length 1.2 to 1.6 in head. Whitish to pink with a lateral yellow stripe at level of upper end of gill opening; median fins yellow. Reaches about 15 inches. Indo-Pacific. Very closely related to *M. martinicus* (Cuvier and Valenciennes) of the Atlantic. Often seen in aggregations in the reef by day, but forages individually at night. Food habits similar to *flavolineatus*. Tends to occur in deeper water on the average than *flavolineatus*. Some authors have mistakenly used the name *auriflamma* for this species (a name now invalidated by the International Commission on Zoological Nomenclature).

55. *Parupeneus pleurostigma* (Bennett), 1830. **sidespot goatfish, malu**
Pectoral rays 15 or 16; gill rakers 29 to 32; depth of body 3.7 to 3.9 in standard length; snout 1.8 to 2.1 in head; barbels relatively short, 1.4 to 1.7 in head, not extending to upper posterior margin of preopercle; last dorsal ray longer than penultimate ray, about equal to first branched ray. Whitish to pink with a black spot about four scales in diameter on lateral line beneath rear of first dorsal fin, followed by a large oval white area; basal third of second dorsal fin blackish. Reaches about 13 inches. Indo-Pacific. Stomach contents of 15 specimens consisted of crabs and crab larvae (36%), polychaete worms (20%), shrimps, heart urchins, peanut worms, pelecypods, foraminifera, brittle stars, fishes, amphipods, mantis shrimps, gastropods, and unidentified crustaceans.

56. *Parupeneus cyclostomus* (Lacepède), 1801.   **blue goatfish, moano kea**
Pectoral rays 16 or 17; gill rakers 29 to 32; depth of body 3.4 to 3.9 in standard length; snout 1.65 to 2 in head; barbels long, extending to or beyond posterior end of head; last dorsal ray longer than penultimate but shorter than first branched ray. Yellowish gray, the scales broadly marked with bright blue; a large saddle-like yellow spot on caudal peduncle; blue bands radiating from eye, and blue bands in second dorsal, anal, and caudal fins. An all-yellow color phase is common outside Hawaii. Reaches about 20 inches. One of 16 inches weighed 3 lbs. Indo-Pacific. Stomach contents of 12 specimens consisted of fishes (70%), peanut worms, shrimps, crabs, octopuses, and small gastropods. *P. chryserydros* (Lacepède) is a synonym.

57. *Parupeneus bifasciatus* (Lacepède), 1801.   **doublebar goatfish, munu**
Pectoral rays 15 or 16; gill rakers 36 to 41; depth of body 2.9 to 3.2 in standard length; snout 1.7 to 2 in head; barbels relatively short, 1.6 to 1.9 in head; last dorsal ray only slightly longer than penultimate ray, shorter than first branched ray. Yellowish gray to reddish with two broad dark bars on body, one centered under anterior part of first dorsal fin and the other beneath posterior part of second dorsal fin; a third fainter bar sometimes present dorsally on caudal peduncle (bars more evident on juveniles than adults). Reaches about 13 inches. Indo-Pacific. The stomachs of 17 specimens were opened (five empty) which revealed feeding on crabs (44%), shrimps, octopuses, mantis shrimps, amphipods, other crustaceans, fishes, and polychaetes. More with food in early morning hours, suggesting heavier feeding at night when the level of illumination is low.

58. *Parupeneus multifasciatus* (Quoy and Gaimard), 1825.

                                                  manybar goatfish, moano
Pectoral rays 15 to 17; gill rakers 37 to 42; depth of body 3 to 3.8 in standard length; snout 1.7 to 1.9 in head; barbels relatively long, 1.1. to 1.3 in head, reaching beyond preopercle; last dorsal ray notably the longest. Reddish with two broad blackish bars in middle of body (one centered beneath interdorsal space and the other beneath second dorsal fin), one on caudal peduncle, and a fourth more diffuse one from nape to below pectoral base; a horizontally elongate blackish spot behind eye. Largest Bishop Museum specimen, 11.3 inches. A fully mature female measures only 7.2 inches. Found only in the Pacific Ocean from near shore to at least 450 feet. Stomach contents of 14 consisted of crabs (including raninids) (46%), shrimps (30%), other crustaceans, fishes, damselfish eggs, octopuses, pelecypods, gastropods, and foraminifera.

59. *Parupeneus porphyreus* (Jenkins), 1903.   **whitesaddle goatfish, kūmū**
Pectoral rays 14 to 16 (usually 15); gill rakers 31 to 34; depth of body 2.8 to 3.1 in standard length; snout 1.8 to 2.1 in head; barbels relatively short, 1.7 to 1.9 in head; last dorsal ray about equal to or shorter than penultimate ray, much shorter than first branched ray. Olivaceous to red (depending on depth, more red occurring on deeper-dwelling fish), shading to whitish ventrally, with a distinct white saddle-like spot dorsally on caudal peduncle just behind base of second dorsal fin; a diffuse dark bar on peduncle behind white spot; an indistinct diagonal dark band on snout through eye to beneath first dorsal containing a darker spot between eye and upper end of gill opening; an adjacent pale band beneath dark band; fins red. Attains about 15 inches. Hawaiian Islands. Young common on reefs inshore; adults have been sighted from a submarine in depths to 460 feet. Feeds on crabs, shrimps, isopods, amphipods, foraminifera, and mantis shrimps, with occasional ingestion of fishes, mollusks, ostracods, polychaetes, and other crustaceans.

BUTTERFLYFISHES (CHAETODONTIDAE)

Perhaps more than any other group of fishes the butterflyfishes add that final exotic touch to the beauty of the coral reefs of tropic seas just as butterflies complete the esthetic picture of a tropical rainforest. The family is well represented in Hawaii with 22 species. These colorful fishes are high-bodied and strongly compressed; they have small protractile mouths with a band of brush-like teeth in the jaws; there are no teeth on the roof of the mouth; the ctenoid scales cover the head, body and median fins; there is a single dorsal fin with no notch between the spinous and soft portions; the dorsal spines, which vary in number from VI to XVI, are stout, the membranes of the anterior spines deeply incised; anal spines III to V, also stout; the caudal fin varies in shape from emarginate to slightly rounded. The late postlarval stage of butterflyfishes, called the tholichthys larva, has large bony plates over the head and anterior body. Most butterflyfishes are diurnal; at night they are at rest on the bottom, though generally alert. Many exhibit a color change at night. The majority of the chaetodontid fishes are complexly colored. Most have a dark bar on the head which tends to obliterate the eye, but in addition they are variously barred, striped or have large isolated spots. These color patterns have probably evolved principally for species recognition. Many of the species of the large genus *Chaetodon* feed on the polyps of corals or on other coelenterates; also significant in the diet of some species are filamentous algae, polychaete worms, and zooplankton. With the exception of a few deep-water species and a few others with little depth preference, the chaetodontid fishes are shallow-water reef species. Obviously those that eat coral polyps or benthic algae are not apt to stray into deeper water where the growth of reef-building corals and algae is poor. Although some of these fishes may be seen in aggregations, most are encountered as solitary individuals or in pairs. A few obligate coral polyp feeding species have been shown to occupy restricted territories on reefs which they defend. Many others have demonstrable home ranges. Two general Hawaiian names, kikākapu and lau-hau, are applied to all but a few of the chaetodontid fishes in Hawaii, as might be expected for species with relatively little value as food fishes. Omitted from this book are the deep-water species *Chaetodon modestus* Temminck and Schlegel and the rare *C. citrinellus* (Cuvier and Valenciennes), *Megaprotodon trifascialis* (Gmelin), and *Hemitaurichthys thompsoni* Fowler.

60. *Chaetodon auriga* **Forsskål, 1775.**　　　　**threadfin butterflyfish, kikākapu**
Dorsal rays XIII,23 to 25; anal rays III,19 to 21; pectoral rays 16; fourth to sixth dorsal rays of adults prolonged into a filament which extends beyond caudal fin; snout produced; caudal fin slightly rounded. White with two series of diagonal dark lines at right angles, shading posteriorly to orange-yellow; a black bar through eye (very broad below eye) and a black spot in upper posterior part of dorsal fin. Largest Bishop Museum specimen, 7.8 inches. Indo-Pacific. Feeds mainly on polychaetes, coral polyps, and algae.

61. *Chaetodon ephippium* **Cuvier and Valenciennes, 1831.**
　　　　　　　　　　　　　　　　saddleback butterflyfish, kikākapu
Dorsal rays XIII,23 to 25; anal rays III,21 to 23; pectoral rays 16; fourth to sixth dorsal rays of adults prolonged to a filament which extends beyond caudal fin; snout produced, the lower jaw strongly projecting; caudal fin truncate to slightly emarginate. Light purplish gray with a large black area on upper posterior part of body extending broadly into dorsal fin; black area rimmed with white below and yellow and orange posteriorly; purple stripes on ventral half of body; lower part of head, chest, and pelvic fins orange-yellow. Largest Bishop Museum specimen, 8.2 inches. Central and western Pacific. Not common in Hawaii. Feeds principally on coral polyps and filamentous algae.

62. *Chaetodon quadrimaculatus* Gray, 1833. fourspot butterflyfish, lau-hau
Dorsal rays XIV,21 or 22; anal rays III,16 to 18; pectoral rays 15 to 17; caudal fin
rounded. Upper half of body dark brown with two white spots on upper side, lower half
orange-yellow with a small brown spot on each scale (a narrow zone of yellow extending
upward to enclose more posterior white spot); a narrow blue band in dorsal and anal fins.
Maximum length about 6 inches. Oceania, mainly in outer reef areas. Feeds primarily on
coral polyps. Frequently swims in pairs.

63. *Chaetodon lunula* (Lacepède), 1802. raccoon butterflyfish, kikākapu
Dorsal rays XII,23 or 24; anal rays III,17 to 19; pectoral rays 17, caudal fin rounded.
Orange-yellow, dusky on upper half of body, with narrow diagonal dark brown or
brownish red bands; a broad black ocular bar followed by one of white; a broad
yellow-edged black wedge from upper gill opening to dorsal fin at base of eighth dorsal
spine; anterior caudal peduncle crossed by a broad yellow-edged black band which
continues upward as a dusky arc basally in dorsal fin. Reaches nearly 8 inches. Indo-
Pacific. Found more on exposed reefs than other chaetodontids but also occurs in
protected waters; the young often seen in tidepools. Nocturnal; feeds on opisthobranch
gastropods, tubeworm tentacles and a great variety of other invertebrates; feeding on
coral polyps and algae is also reported.

64. *Chaetodon miliaris* Quoy and Gaimard, 1824.
  milletseed butterflyfish, lau-wiliwili
Dorsal rays XIII,21 to 23; anal rays III,19 to 21; pectoral rays 15 or 16; caudal fin
truncate. Yellow with vertical rows of small blackish spots on upper two-thirds of body, a
black ocular bar, and a broad black zone on caudal peduncle and caudal base. Attains 6.5
inches. Endemic to the Hawaiian Islands where it is the most common species of the
family. Seems closest to *Chaetodon guntheri* Ahl from the western Pacific. Inshore to
600 feet. Feeds mainly on zooplankton; also occasionally a cleaner. Second only to *C.
multicinctus* among the species of *Chaetodon* in the number landed for the aquarium fish
trade. Sometimes called the lemon butterflyfish.

65. *Chaetodon fremblii* Bennett, 1829. bluestripe butterflyfish, kikākapu
Dorsal rays XIV (rarely XIII),20 to 22; anal rays III,16 to 18; pectoral rays 16 (rarely 15);
caudal fin truncate. Yellow with eight slightly diagonal blue stripes on body, three of which
converge to eye, and another in dorsal and anal fins; no black ocular bar; a black spot
dorsally on nape in front of dorsal fin and a large black area on caudal peduncle extending
dorsally into dorsal fin. Largest Bishop Museum specimen, 6 inches. Restricted to the
Hawaiian Islands where it is a common species. Appears to be a relic species. Preys on
the tentacles of tubeworms and a variety of other invertebrates.

66. *Chaetodon kleinii* Bloch, 1790. blacklip butterflyfish, kikākapu
Dorsal rays XIII,21 or 22; anal rays III,18 or 19; pectoral rays 14 or 15; caudal fin
truncate. Body orange-yellow, the centers of the scales whitish, with two diffuse broad
brown bars, one anteriorly and one in about middle of body; a black ocular bar; pelvic fins
largely dark brown. A small species, it reaches a maximum of about 4.5 inches.
Indo-Pacific. Common below about 60 feet. Feeds mainly on zooplankton. *C. corallicola*
Snyder is a synonym.

67. *Chaetodon lineolatus* Cuvier and Valenciennes, 1831.
  lined butterflyfish, kikākapu
Dorsal rays XII,24 to 27; anal rays III,19 to 22; pectoral rays 17 or 18; snout produced,
2.3 to 2.6 in head; caudal fin slightly rounded. White with vertical black lines; a broad

diagonal black band on back beneath posterior half of dorsal fin extending across caudal peduncle and narrowing onto anal fin base, the upper part of band with a zone of yellow below; a broad black ocular bar; median fins largely yellow. The largest member of the genus; longest specimen examined, 11.7 inches. Indo-Pacific. Not common. Observed from a submarine at depths to 560 feet in Hawaii. May be seen as solitary fish or in pairs.

68. *Chaetodon ornatissimus* Cuvier and Valenciennes, 1831.

ornate butterflyfish, kīkākapu

Dorsal rays XII,25 to 27; anal rays III,20 to 22; pectoral rays 16 or 17; caudal fin rounded; snout somewhat blunt, 2.7 to 3.1 in head. Body white with six diagonal orange bands; head and nape yellow with five black bars, one of which extends into dorsal fin for its entire length; two black bands in caudal and anal fins. Attains 8 inches. Central and western Pacific. Feeds mainly on coral polyps. Often swims in pairs.

69. *Chaetodon trifasciatus* Mungo Park, 1797.   **oval butterflyfish, kapuhili**

Dorsal rays XIII,21 or 22; anal rays III,19 or 20; pectoral rays 15 or 16; snout short, 3 to 3.4 in head; caudal fin rounded. Yellow-orange with slightly diagonal narrow purplish stripes; front of snout black, separated from black ocular bar by yellow; ocular bar followed by yellow and narrow white and black bars; dorsal fin mainly white with light red on outer soft portion; a yellow-edged black band below posterior portion of dorsal fin, extending onto upper caudal peduncle; soft anal with a yellow-edged black band basally, most of fin dark red; caudal fin white with yellow-edged black bar. To 5.5 inches. Indo-Pacific. Found mainly on coral reefs in bays or lagoons where it feeds principally on coral polyps. Exhibits a strong pair bond.

70. *Chaetodon unimaculatus* Bloch, 1787.   **teardrop butterflyfish, lau-hau**

Dorsal rays XIII,22 or 23; anal rays III,19 or 20; pectoral rays 15 or 16; caudal fin truncate. Body yellow dorsally, shading to white on sides, with a large white-edged black spot centered on middle of lateral line (some blackish pigment extending and narrowing downward from spot); vertical lines of yellow on body anterior to spot reaching to beneath pectoral fin; broad black ocular bar; dorsal and anal fins yellow except posteriorly where black with a white margin; caudal fin whitish. Largest Bishop Museum specimen, 7.8 inches. Indo-Pacific. In feeding on coral polyps it often ingests some of the calices; also consumes soft corals, polychaetes, small crustaceans, and filamentous algae. Commonly seen in pairs.

71. *Chaetodon multicinctus* Garrett, 1863.   **multiband butterflyfish, kīkākapu**

Dorsal rays XIII,24 to 26; anal rays III,18 or 19; pectoral rays 15 or 16 (usually 15); caudal fin slightly rounded. White with six light brown bars on body, speckled with small spots of olive-brown (spots larger and darker within bars); dark ocular bar (brown below, black above) interrupted on forehead; caudal peduncle crossed by a black bar, and another half way out in caudal fin. To about 4 inches. Found only in the Hawaiian Islands. The fifth most important species of the aquarium fish trade in Hawaii. Coral polyps are its principal food. Usually observed swimming in pairs. The allopatric *C. punctatofasciatus* Cuvier and Valenciennes of the central and western Pacific seems to be the closest relative.

72. *Chaetodon reticulatus* Cuvier and Valenciennes, 1831.

reticulated butterflyfish

Dorsal rays XII (rarely XIII),27 or 28; anal rays III,21 or 22; pectoral rays 16 or 17 (usually 17); caudal fin rounded. Body posterior to pectoral base black with a yellowish spot on each scale except posteriorly on caudal peduncle and caudal fin base where solid black; a broad zone of light gray anteriorly on body and on posterior head, becoming yellowish on chest where it narrows to pelvic base; a broad black bar edged in yellow through eye, the lower part curving to base of pelvic fins; chin and snout black with a narrow yellow band running anteriorly from eye; dorsal fin gray with a narrow white margin and broad light yellow submarginal band on soft portion of fin; anal fin black with a narrow white margin and a median yellowish band except posteriorly in distal part of fin where there is a broad zone of bright red; caudal fin black basally, gray centrally, with a black-edged yellow band on distal margin; pectoral fins pale, pelvic fins black. Attains about 7 inches. Distribution confined to the Pacific from French Polynesia and the Pitcairn Group to the Ryukyus and Philippines. Rare in the Hawaiian Islands; most often seen at the island of Hawaii. A facultative coral polyp feeder; occasionally grazes heavily on filamentous algae.

73. *Chaetodon tinkeri* **Schultz, 1951.** **Tinker's butterflyfish**
Dorsal rays XIII (rarely XIV),20 to 22; anal rays III,16 or 17; pectoral rays 15; caudal fin slightly rounded; third and fourth dorsal spines notably the longest, the remaining spines diminishing in length; soft portion of dorsal fin also low with no angular portion posteriorly, the rays extending to or only slightly beyond a vertical at caudal fin base (in contrast to other Hawaiian *Chaetodon*). Head white with a yellow bar through eye and a yellow spot on front of snout; body white with a small blackish spot on each scale up to a diagonal passing from base of fourth dorsal spine through base of tenth anal soft ray where the color becomes abruptly black, this continuing onto most of dorsal fin and posterior part of the anal fin; dorsal fin with a white margin, black submarginal line, and below this a yellow band which broadens on the anterior spines (the three most anterior spines mainly white); anterior two-thirds of anal fin and paired fins white; a small blotch of yellow distally on anal fin at demarcation of the black and white colors and another at upper base of pectoral fin; caudal fin yellow. Attains about 5½ inches. Believed endemic to the Hawaiian Islands until recently when a specimen was collected at Enewetak, Marshall Islands. Rarely seen in less than 100 feet. In spite of its preference for deep water, it does very well in aquaria. A major factor contributing to its success in aquaria is its catholic food habits. Its closest relatives such as *C. mitratus* Günther from the Indian Ocean, *C. declivis* Randall from the Marquesas, and *C. flavocoronatus* Myers from Guam are also species of moderately deep water.

74. *Hemitaurichthys polylepis* **Bleeker, 1857.** **pyramid butterflyfish**
Dorsal rays XII,24 or 25; anal rays III,19 to 21; pectoral rays 18 or 19; lateral line complete (in contrast to *Chaetodon* on which the lateral line ends beneath rear of dorsal fin); snout slightly produced, but short, 2.7 to 3.2 in head; pelvic fins filamentous, reaching beyond origin of anal fin (not reaching anal fin on Hawaiian *Chaetodon*); caudal fin truncate. Head and body anterior to base of third dorsal spine brown, the rest yellow and white (the white in a broad central triangular zone with apex at base of ninth dorsal spine, encompassing caudal peduncle, caudal fin, and paired fins). Reaches about 6 inches. Central and western Pacific. Often seen in aggregations; feeds on zooplankton. Although usually found in more than 50 feet, it may occur in as little as 20 feet. Sometimes called the brownface butterflyfish. The related *H. zoster* (Bennett) of the Indian Ocean is dark brown with a broad middle bar of white that converges only slightly dorsally.

75. *Heniochus diphreutes* **Jordan, 1903.** **pennantfish**
Dorsal rays XII,23 to 25; anal rays III,17 to 19; pectoral rays 16 to 18; fourth dorsal spine and associated membranous filament exceedingly long, normally extending beyond caudal fin; lateral line complete, the pored scales 46 to 54; caudal fin truncate. White with two broad diagonal black bands, the first from origin of dorsal fin to abdomen, continuing onto pelvic fins, and the second from mid-spinous dorsal fin to posterior anal fin; soft dorsal, caudal, and pectoral fins yellow. To at least 8 inches. Recorded from southern

Japan, Hawaii, east and west coasts of Australia, Maldive Islands, Natal coast of South Africa, and the Red Sea. Usually seen in aggregations well above the substratum; feeds mainly on zooplankton; the author has observed it clean other fishes. Occurs in various habitats from shallow bays and lagoons to outer reef areas; on exposed coasts generally found in more than 50 feet; deepest collection, 500 feet; submarine observations to 600 feet. A popular aquarium fish. Closely related to the bannerfish, *H. acuminatus* (Linnaeus), which is almost identical in form and coloration but differs in having XI dorsal spines and 25 to 27 dorsal soft rays. The latter is more tropical in distribution; it is not known from Hawaii, *(H. diphreutes* is found mainly in warm temperate and subtropical seas.) Also *H. acuminatus* is solitary fish as an adult, or occurs in pairs, and swims near the bottom. In contrast to *H. diphreutes,* it is closely tied to coral reefs.

76. *Forcipiger flavissimus* **Jordan and McGregor, 1898.**

forcepsfish, lau-wiliwili-nukunuku-'oi'oi

Dorsal rays XII (rarely XI),21 to 25; anal rays III,17 to 19; pectoral rays 15 to 17; lateral line complete; snout extremely slender and elongate, more than half length of head, 3.6 to 4.5 in standard length; gape 1.3 to 3.4 in eye; pelvic fins filamentous, reaching beyond origin of anal fin; caudal fin slightly emarginate to truncate. Body, dorsal, anal, and pelvic fins yellow; nape and upper half of head black, lower half of head and thorax white; a large black spot posteriorly in anal fin. Largest Bishop Museum specimen, 7.2 inches. Indo-Pacific and tropical eastern Pacific. Feeds on polychaetes (especially the tentacles of tubeworms) and other worms, pedicellariae and tubefeet of sea urchins, mysid shrimps, amphipods, other small crustaceans, barnacle cirri, and fish eggs. The second most important fish in Hawaii of the commercial aquarium fish trade.

77. *Forcipiger longirostris* **Broussonet, 1782.**

longnose butterflyfish, lau-wiliwili-nukunuku-'oi'oi

Dorsal rays XI (rarely X),24 to 28; anal rays III,17 to 20; pectoral rays 15 to 17; lateral line complete; snout enormously produced, much more than half length of head, 2.6 to 3 in standard length; mouth with a very short gape, 4.3 to 6 in eye diameter; pelvic fins very long and filamentous, reaching well beyond origin of anal fin; caudal fin emarginate, the upper lobe significantly longer than the lower. Occurs in two diverse color phases, one almost identical to *F. flavissimus,* differing in having a median black band on top of snout and small blackish spots in the centers of the scales on the chest, and the other dark brown except base of caudal fin and base and axil of pectoral fins which are yellow. Largest Bishop Museum specimen, 8.6 inches. Widespread in the Indo-Pacific but known from fewer localities than *F. flavissimus.* Not common in less than about 60 feet; tends to range into deeper water, on the average, than *F. flavissimus. F. longirostris* was the first fish described from the Hawaiian Islands; it was collected on Capt. James Cook's third voyage in "Resolution" (1776-1780). Feeds principally on very small free-living crustaceans. *F. cyrano* Randall and *F. inornatus* Randall are synonyms, the latter based on the dark color phase.

ANGELFISHES (POMACANTHIDAE)

Formerly the angelfishes were grouped by most ichthyologists as a subfamily of the Chaetodontidae, but they are now considered a separate family. Although they share most of the general characters given for the butterflyfishes such as a deep compressed body, small ctenoid scales which extend onto the median fins, small mouth with brush-like dentition, and a single unnotched dorsal fin, there are noteworthy differences. The pomacanthids are distinctive in possessing a prominent large spine at the corner of the preopercle (as well as lesser spines on the preopercle, interopercle, and preorbital); they lack a scaly axillary process at the base of the pelvic fins; the scales are more strongly ctenoid with distinct ridges along the exposed part of the scale leading to each little tooth at the margin, and adults have auxiliary scales; they lack the anterior bifurcation of the swim bladder that is characteristic of chaetodontids; their postlarvae do not have bony plates over the head and anterior body. Eight angelfishes occur in the Hawaiian Islands: five species of *Centropyge* (the Hawaiian records of two of these, *C. multicolor* Randall and Wass from the island of Hawaii and *C. interruptus* (Tanaka) from the leeward Hawaiian Islands, are based on single specimens), the endemic *Holacanthus arcuatus* Gray, *Genicanthus personatus* Randall (also native to Hawaii), and *Pomacanthus imperator* (Bloch). *G. personatus* is known from only six specimens collected in the depth range of 80 to 275 feet. The record of *P. imperator* (popularly called the emperor angelfish) is based on a single specimen collected in 1948, hence probably not an aquarium release (the recent sighting of a juvenile off Oahu also suggests natural occurrence). The species of *Centropyge,* all relatively small fishes, feed on filamentous algae and detritus. They have restricted home ranges and stay close to cover. Recent research in Japan has shown that *C. interruptus* (and hence perhaps all *Centropyge*) undergoes sex reversal from female to male. Females outnumber males, and males maintain harems. Sex reversal has also been shown for *Genicanthus,* and the preponderance of females suggests that males of the species of this genus may also have harems. The species of *Genicanthus* seem to feed mainly on zooplankton. The species of *Holacanthus* and *Pomacanthus* are primarily sponge feeders. Some of the angelfishes, especially those of the genus *Pomacanthus,* have dramatically different color patterns as juveniles. The generic classification needs revision.

78. *Holacanthus arcuatus* Gray, 1831.   **bandit angelfish**

Dorsal rays XIII,17 or 18; anal rays III,18; pectoral rays 17 or 18; depth of body 1.65 to 1.9 in standard length; no enlarged spines on preorbital; caudal fin rounded. A broad black band from snout through eye to posterior dorsal fin; back above band olive, each scale with a white spot; head and body below band white; anal fin largely black with white border; caudal fin with a broad black submarginal band. Reaches about 7 inches. Found only in the Hawaiian Islands. Not common. Usually occurs in more than 40 feet; submarine observations to 430 feet. Stomachs of ten specimens contained sponges (91%), algae, traces of hydroids, and unidentified eggs.

79. *Centropyge potteri* (Jordan and Metz), 1912.   **Potter's angelfish**

Dorsal rays XIV,16 to 18; anal rays III,17 or 18; pectoral rays 17 (rarely 18); depth of body 1.75 to 2 in standard length; no enlarged spines on preorbital; caudal fin rounded. Irregular narrow bars of grayish blue and orange on head and body except for a broad central region of body and posterior dorsal and anal fins where blackish replaces the orange; extreme posterior dorsal, anal, and caudal fins with alternating bands of black and light blue paralleling rays; paired fins yellow. Attains 5 inches. Confined to the Hawaiian Islands. The most common of Hawaiian angelfishes and among the more common reef fishes, in general. The third most important commercial species of the aquarium fish trade in Hawaii. Peak reproductive activity occurs from mid-December through May. Spawning takes place at dusk during the week preceding full moon.

80. *Centropyge fisheri* (Snyder), 1904.   **Fisher's angelfish**

Dorsal rays XIV,16; anal rays III,16 or 17; pectoral rays 16 (rarely 17); depth of body 2 to 2.1 in standard length; two or three greatly enlarged spines on preorbital; caudal fin truncate to slightly rounded. Orange, overlaid with brown in broad central region of body; a large bluish black spot above pectoral base at edge of gill opening; caudal and pectoral fins yellowish; anterior margin of pelvic and anal fins blue. To 3 inches. Hawaiian Islands, generally in more than 80 feet. Often associated with rubble bottom. *C. flavicauda* Fraser-Brunner from elsewhere in the central and western Pacific is a close relative.

81. *Centropyge loriculus* (Günther), 1873.   **flame angelfish**
Dorsal rays XIV,16 to 18; anal rays III,17 or 18; pectoral rays 17 or 18 (rarely 18); depth of body 1.8 to 2.05 in standard length; two or three spines on preorbital may be slightly enlarged; caudal fin rounded. Bright red with three to seven black bars on side of body, the first broader and shorter (occasional bars double or branched); black spots often present on back or dorsal fin above bars; posterior dorsal and anal fins banded with purple and black. Largest of 58 Bishop Museum specimens (collected from 5 to 190 feet), 3.9 inches. Oceania. Rare in Hawaii; a highly prized aquarium fish. *C. flammeus* Schultz is a synonym.

DAMSELFISHES (POMACENTRIDAE)

The damselfishes (or demoiselles) are among the most abundant of reef fishes. The most distinctive family feature is the single nasal opening on each side of the snout (most fishes have two). The mouth is small, and when closed, the maxilla is not fully exposed on the cheek; the dentition is varied (though none have any teeth on the roof of the mouth). The lateral line is incomplete, ending below rear of dorsal fin. There is a single dorsal fin of X to XIV spines, the base of the spinous portion longer than the soft; anal spines II; the caudal fin usually forked. Fourteen species of damselfishes are known from the Hawaiian Islands, of which seven are *Chromis*. Species accounts are not provided for the two deep-water chromis, *C. leucura* Gilbert and *C. struhsakeri* Randall and Swerdloff. The *Chromis, Dascyllus albisella,* and *Abudefduf abdominalis* feed mainly on zooplankton; these species often occur in aggregations. The remaining Hawaiian damselfishes are more closely associated with the bottom; they are generally omnivorous, solitary, and highly territorial. Because of their pugnacity, they are not ideal aquarium fishes, especially as adults. Damselfish eggs are elliptical in shape, attached at one end to hard substratum or benthic algae; the patches of eggs, termed nests, are guarded by the male parent. The young of some damselfishes are more colorful than adults.

82. *Abudefduf sordidus* (Forsskål), 1775.   **blackspot sergeant, kūpīpī**
Dorsal rays XIII,15 or 16 (usually 15); anal rays, II,14 or 15; pectoral rays 18 or 19 (usually 19); tubed lateral-line scales 21 or 22; depth of body 1.5 to 1.9; short incisiform teeth in a single row in jaws, trifid in young, bifid in larger individuals, and smoothly rounded to truncate in large adults; margin of preopercle smooth. Light yellowish, the edges of the scales brown, shading to dirty white on lower side, with seven dark brown bars, the first on nape and the last on caudal fin base; a black spot larger than eye dorsally on caudal peduncle just behind base of dorsal fin; a small black spot at upper base of pectoral fin. Largest Bishop Museum specimen, 9.3 inches. Indo-Pacific. An inshore species of rocky bottom, often where surge is strong. Young common in tidepools. The diet is varied, some stomachs with algae, others with crabs and other crustaceans (including barnacle appendages), sponges, polychaete worms, etc.

83. *Abudefduf abdominalis* (Quoy and Gaimard), 1825. Hawaiian sergeant, mamo
Dorsal rays XIII,13 to 15; anal rays II,13 to 15; pectoral rays 17 to 19; tubed lateral-line scales 21 or 22; depth of body 1.7 to 2 in standard length; dentition similar to *A. sordidus*; preopercle smooth. Light blue-green, the edges of the scales yellow, shading to white ventrally; five black bars on body (the fifth on caudal peduncle usually faint); a large

blackish spot at rear base of dorsal and anal fins; a small black spot at upper pectoral base. Largest Bishop Museum specimen, 9.8 inches, from Laysan. Restricted to the Hawaiian Islands, where it is abundant. The only Hawaiian member of a complex of closely related species which includes *A. saxatilis* (Linnaeus). Found in more protected waters than *A. sordidus* (if inshore, in sheltered water; off exposed coasts, in deeper water). The young occur in tidepools or other calm shallow habitats. Feeds mainly on zooplankton, particularly copepods, but a significant amount of algae is ingested. Spawning is year-around, but there is increased reproductive activity from mid-December through July. Spawning sites have been observed from near the surface to 90 feet. During breeding the males become pale blue, and the black bars fade to pale gray. The eggs are usually red initially, average 1.3 mm in length, and are laid on a hard substratum in a roughly circular patch about 9 inches in diameter. Hatching takes place early on the sixth day. The duration of larval life is 3 to 4 weeks (depending on temperature); newly transformed juveniles average 0.5 to 0.6 inches. They grow at a rate of about 10 mm (0.4 inches) per month.

84. *Plectroglyphidodon imparipennis* **(Vaillant and Sauvage) 1875.**

brighteye damselfish

Dorsal rays XII,14 to 16; anal rays II,11 or 12; pectoral rays 19 or 20; tubed lateral-line scales 19; depth of body 2.1 to 2.3 in standard length; dorsal profile of head convex; maxilla reaching a vertical at front of eye; teeth in a single row, long and slender, close-set, protruding, the tips rounded; margin of preopercle smooth. Yellowish gray, shading to white ventrally and to light yellow posteriorly; no black markings except a black bar in eye above and slightly below pupil (iris otherwise light yellow). Reaches about 2.5 inches. Indo-Pacific. A common inshore species of exposed rocky coasts, always found close to the substratum. Feeds on a wide variety of small invertebrate animals, but especially polychaete worms and small crustaceans. Often classified in the genus *Abudefduf* (along with the following two species).

85. *Plectroglyphidodon johnstonianus* **Fowler and Ball, 1924.**

blue-eye damselfish

Dorsal rays XII,18 (rarely 19); anal rays II,16 or 17; pectoral rays 19; tubed lateral-line scales 21 or 22; depth of body 1.7 to 1.8 in standard length; dorsal profile of head nearly straight; maxilla not reaching vertical at front of eye; posterior portion of preorbital scaled; lips fleshy, vertically furrowed; teeth similar to *P. imparipennis* but the tips sharper and slightly incurved; preopercular margin smooth or partially crenulate. Yellowish, usually with a large vertically elongate blackish area nearly crossing body below posterior part of dorsal fin; faint blue spots on head; iris blue. Largest Bishop Museum specimen, 4.7 inches. Indo-Pacific. Generally associated with live coral; feeds heavily on the polyps.

86. *Plectroglyphidodon sindonis* **(Jordan and Evermann), 1903. rock damselfish**

Dorsal rays XII,19 or 20; anal rays II,15 or 16; pectoral rays 21; tubed lateral-line scales 21 or 22; depth of body 1.6 to 1.7 in standard length (less depth in juveniles, to 1.9 in standard length); maxilla nearly reaching a vertical at front edge of eye; teeth in a single row, long and slender, close-set, the tips bluntly pointed; margin of preopercle smooth. Dark brown, the edges of the scales darker than centers; two narrow whitish bars near center of body; a triangular black spot at upper pectoral base; juveniles with a round black spot about twice as large as eye anteriorly at base of soft portion of dorsal fin and extending half onto back, this spot nearly encircled by a pale band which is continuous with second whitish bar on body. Reaches 5 inches. Known only from the Hawaiian Islands. Occurs in very shallow water in the surge zone of exposed rocky shores. Feeds mainly on benthic algae, occasionally on small invertebrates.

1.
variegated lizardfish
Synodus variegatus
'ulae
6.7 in. (170 mm)

2.
twospot lizardfish
Synodus binotatus
'ulae
6.3 in. (160 mm)

3.
orangemouth lizardfish
Saurida flamma
'ulae
12.2 in. (310 mm)

4.
mustache conger
Conger cinereus
pūhi-ūhā
34.0 in. (864 mm)

5. **whitemouth moray,** *Gymnothorax meleagris,* pūhi-'ōni'o, 19.7 in. (500 mm)

6. **yellowmargin moray,** *Gymnothorax flavimarginatus,* pūhi-paka, 31.7 in. (805 mm)

7. **stout moray,** *Gymnothorax eurostus,* pūhi, 17.5 in. (444 mm)

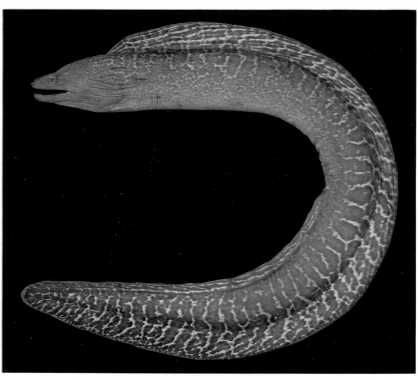

8. **undulated moray,** *Gymnothorax undulatus,* pūhi-lau-milo, 25.2 in. (640 mm)

9. **snowflake moray**
Echidna nebulosa
pūhi-kāpā
27.7 in. (703 mm)

10. **zebra moray**
Gymnomuraena zebra
pūhi
26.2 in. (665 mm)

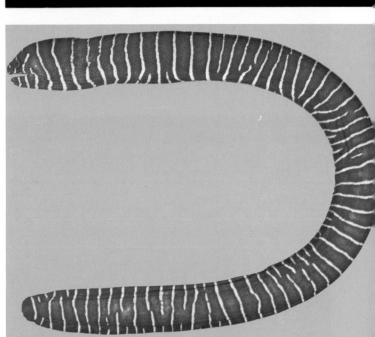

11. **trumpet**
Aulostomus chine
n
18.5 in. (470 r

12. **bluestripe pipe**
Doryhamphus e
2.0 in. (51

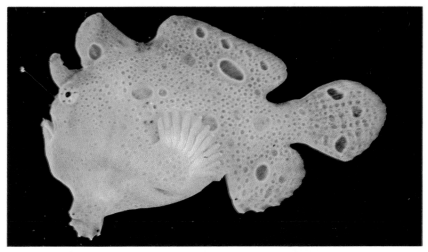

13. Commerson's frogfish, *Antennarius commersonii*, 2.5 in. (63 mm)

14. spotfin squirrelfish, *Neoniphon sammara*, ʻalaʻihi, 7.3 in. (185 mm)

15. peppered squirrelfish, *Sargocentron punctatissimum*, ʻalaʻihi, 4.6 in. (117 mm)

16. **crown squirrelfish,** *Sargocentron diadema,* ʻalaʻihi, 4.3 in. (109 mm)

17. **Hawaiian squirrelfish,** *Sargocentron xantherythrum,* ʻalaʻihi, 5.2 in. (132 mm)

18. **Tahitian squirrelfish,** *Sargocentron tiere,* ʻalaʻihi, 10.2 in. (259 mm)

19. bigscale soldierfish, *Myripristis berndti,* 'ū'ū, 6.6 in. (168 mm)

20. brick soldierfish, *Myripristis amaena,* 'ū'ū, 6.3 in. (160 mm)

21. shoulderbar soldierfish, *Myripristis kuntee,* 'ū'ū, 6.3 in. (160 mm)

22. **speckled scorpionfish,** *Sebastapistes coniorta,* 2.3 in. (58 mm)

23. **spotfin scorpionfish,** *Sebastapistes ballieui,* 3.2 in. (81 mm)

24. **lowfin scorpionfish,** *Scorpaenodes parvipinnis,* 3.4 in. (86 mm)

25. devil scorpionfish, *Scorpaenopsis diabolus,* nohu 'omakaha, 8.5 in. (216 mm)

26. titan scorpionfish, *Scorpaenopsis cacopsis,* nohu, 11.1 in. (282 mm)

27. leaf scorpionfish, *Taenianotus triacanthus,* 1.7 in. (43 mm)

28. decoy scorpionfish, *Iracundus signifer*, 4.8 in. (122 mm)

29. Hawaiian lionfish, *Dendrochirus barberi*, 5.5 in. (140 mm)

30. Hawaiian turkeyfish, *Pterois sphex*, 7.6 in. (193 mm)

31. Hawaiian anthias, *Anthias thompsoni,* 7.0 in. (178 mm)

32. Hawaiian flagtail, *Kuhlia sandvicensis,* āholehole, 6.3 in. (160 mm)

33. glasseye, *Heteropriacanthus cruentatus,* 'āweoweo, 10.3 in. (262 mm)

34. Hawaiian bigeye, *Heteropriacanthus meeki,* 'āweoweo, 11.2 in. (284 mm)

35. iridescent cardinalfish, *Apogon kallopterus,* 'upāpalu, 4.6 in. (117 mm)

36. bandfin cardinalfish, *Apogon taeniopterus,* 'upāpalu, 5.6 in. (142 mm)

37. spotted cardinalfish, *Apogon maculiferus,* 'upāpalu, 2.9 in. (74 mm)

38. Waikiki cardinalfish, *Apogonichthys perdix,* 'upāpalu, 1.8 in. (46 mm)

39. bay cardinalfish, *Foa brachygramma,* 'upāpalu, 3.1 in. (79 mm)

40. Hawaiian morwong, *Cheilodactylus vittatus,* kīkākapu, 10.6 in. (269 mm)

41. **stocky hawkfish,** *Cirrhitus pinnulatus,* poʻo-paʻa, 7.4 in. (188 mm)

42. **blackside hawkfish,** *Paracirrhites forsteri,* hilu pili-koʻa, 5.5 in. (140 mm)

43. **arc-eye hawkfish,** *Paracirrhites arcatus,* pili-koʻa, 2.9 in. (74 mm)

44. redbar hawkfish, *Cirrhitops fasciatus,* pili-koʻa, 3.3 in. (84 mm)

45. twospot hawkfish, *Amblycirrhitus bimacula,* pili-koʻa, 2.7 in. (69 mm)

46. longnose hawkfish, *Oxycirrhites typus,* 3.9 in. (99 mm)

47. bluestripe snapper, *Lutjanus kasmira*, taʻape, 10.8 in. (274 mm)

48. blacktail snapper, *Lutjanus fulvus*, toʻau, 10.5 in. (267 mm)

49. bigeye emperor, *Monotaxis grandoculis*, mū, 10.9 in. (277 mm)

50. **brown chub,** *Kyphosus bigibbus,* nenue, 20.7 in. (526 mm)

51. **lowfin chub,** *Kyphosus vaigiensis,* nenue, 19.0 in. (483 mm)

52. **stripey,** *Microcanthus strigatus,* 5.4 in. (137 mm)

53. yellowstripe goatfish, *Mulloides flavolineatus*, weke, 8.3 in. (211 mm)

54. yellowfin goatfish, *Mulloides vanicolensis*, weke-'ula, 9.7 in. (246 mm)

55. sidespot goatfish, *Parupeneus pleurostigma*, malu, 7.8 in. (198 mm)

56. blue goatfish, *Pseudupeneus cyclostomus*, moano kea, 10.8 in. (274 mm)

57. doublebar goatfish, *Parupeneus bifasciatus*, munu, 9.5 in (241 mm)

58. manybar goatfish, *Parupeneus multifasciatus*, moano, 8.4 in. (213 mm)

59. whitesaddle goatfish, *Parupeneus porphyreus*, kūmū, 11.2 in. (284 mm)

60. threadfin butterflyfish, *Chaetodon auriga,* kīkākapu, 6.8 in. (173 mm)

61. saddleback butterflyfish, *Chaetodon ephippium,* kīkākapu, 7.2 in. (183 mm)

62. fourspot butterflyfish, *Chaetodon quadrimaculatus,* lau-hau, 4.8 in. (122 mm)

63. raccoon butterflyfish, *Chaetodon lunula,* kīkākapu, 5.9 in. (150 mm)

64. milletseed butterflyfish, *Chaetodon miliaris*, lau-wiliwili, 5.9 in. (150 mm)

65. bluestripe butterflyfish, *Chaetodon fremblii*, kīkākapu, 4.5 in. (114 mm)

66. blacklip butterflyfish, *Chaetodon kleinii,* kīkākapu, 4.2 in. (107 mm)

67. lined butterflyfish, *Chaetodon lineolatus,* kīkākapu, 7.3 in. (185 mm)

68. ornate butterflyfish, *Chaetodon ornatissimus,* kīkākapu, 5.4 in. (137 mm)

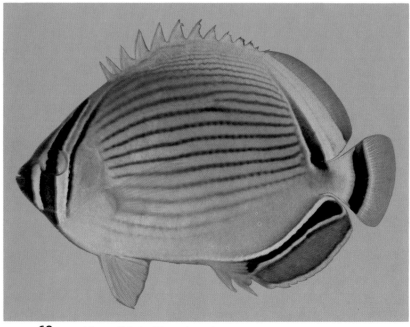

69. oval butterflyfish, *Chaetodon trifasciatus,* kapuhili, 4.6 in. (117 mm)

70. teardrop butterflyfish, *Chaetodon unimaculatus,* lau-hau, 5.0 in. (127 mm)

71. multiband butterflyfish, *Chaetodon multicinctus,* kīkākapu, 3.5 in. (89 mm)

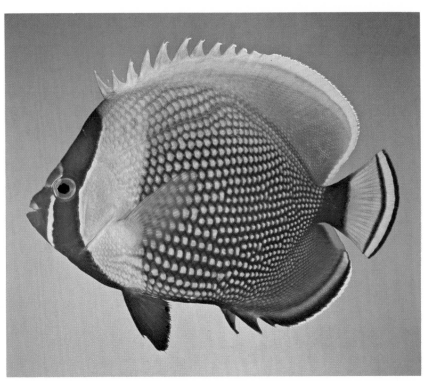

72. reticulated butterflyfish, *Chaetodon reticulatus,* 4.8 in. (122 mm)

73. Tinker's butterflyfish, *Chaetodon tinkeri,* 5.3 in. (135 mm)

74. pyramid butterflyfish, *Hemitaurichthys polylepis*, 5.3 in. (135 mm)

75. pennantfish, *Heniochus diphreutes*, 3.9 in. (99 mm)

76. forcepsfish
Forcipiger flavissimus
lau-wiliwili-nukunuku-ʻoiʻoi
7.0 in. (178 mm)

77. longnose butterflyfish
Forcipiger longirostris
lau-wiliwili-nukunuku-ʻoiʻoi
6.8 in. (173 mm)

78. bandit angelfish, *Holacanthus arcuatus*, 6.5 in (165 mm)

79. **Potter's angelfish,** *Centropyge potteri,* 4.9 in. (124 mm)

80. **Fisher's angelfish,** *Centropyge fisheri,* 1.8 in. (46 mm)

81. **flame angelfish,** *Centropyge loriculus,* 3.0 in. (76 mm)

82. blackspot sergeant, *Abudefduf sordidus*, kūpīpī, 5.1 in. (130 mm)

83. Hawaiian sergeant, *Abudefduf abdominalis*, mamo, 6.4 in. (163 mm)

84. brighteye damselfish, *Plectroglyphidodon imparipennis*, 2.3 in. (58 mm)

85. blue-eye damselfish, *Plectroglyphidodon johnstonianus*, 2.7 in. (69 mm)

86. rock damselfish, *Plectroglyphidodon sindonis*, 4.1 in. (104 mm)

87. Pacific gregory, *Stegastes fasciolatus,* 4.2 in. (107 mm)

88. Hawaiian dascyllus, *Dascyllus albisella,* ʻālo-ʻiloʻi, 4.3 in. (109 mm)

89. chocolate-dip chromis, *Chromis hanui*, 3.8 in. (97 mm)

90. agile chromis, *Chromis agilis*, 3.7 in. (94 mm)

91. oval chromis, *Chromis ovalis*, 6.7 in. (170 mm)

92. threespot chromis, *Chromis verater,* 6.0 in. (152 mm)

93. blackfin chromis, *Chromis vanderbilti,* 2.0 in. (51 mm)

94. rockmover, *Novaculichthys taeniourus,* 7.9 in. (201 mm)

95. ringtail wrasse, *Cheilinus unifasciatus*, pō'ou, 9.7 in. (246 mm)

96a. twospot wrasse, *Cheilinus bimaculatus* ♀, 2.4 in. (61 mm)

96b. twospot wrasse, *Cheilinus bimaculatus* ♂, 4.4 in. (112 mm)

97. Hawaiian cleaner wrasse, *Labroides phthirophagus*, 3.0 in. (76 mm)

98. eightline wrasse, *Pseudocheilinus octotaenia*, 3.9 in. (99 mm)

99. fourline wrasse, *Pseudocheilinus tetrataenia*, 2.7 in. (69 mm)

100a. flame wrasse, *Cirrhilabrus jordani* ♀, 2.0 in. (51 mm)

100b. flame wrasse, *Cirrhilabrus jordani* ♂, 3.5 in. (89 mm)

101a. Hawaiian hogfish, *Bodianus bilunulatus* ♀, 'a'awa, 10.8 in. (274 mm)

101b. Hawaiian hogfish, *Bodianus bilunulatus* ♂, 'a'awa 17.5 in. (444 mm)

102a. lined coris, *Coris ballieui* ♀, mālamalama, 7.2 in. (183 mm)

102b. lined coris, *Coris ballieui* ♂, mālamalama, 9.0 in. (229 mm)

103. elegant coris, *Coris venusta,* 5.5 in. (140 mm)

104a. yellowstripe coris, *Coris flavovittata* juv., hilu, 3.0 in. (76 mm)

104b. yellowstripe coris, *Coris flavovittata* ♀, hilu, 7.3 in. (185 mm)

104c. yellowstripe coris, *Coris flavovittata* ♂, hilu, 18.5 in. (470 mm)

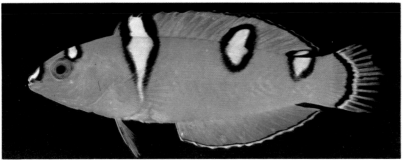

105a. yellowtail coris, *Coris gaimard* juv., hīnālea-ʻaki-lolo, 2.1 in. (53 mm)

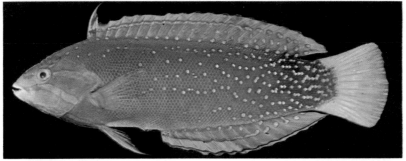

105b. yellowtail coris, *Coris gaimard* ♀, hīnālea-ʻaki-lolo, 6.1 in. (155 mm)

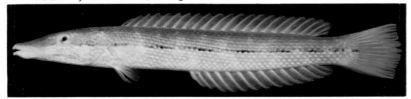

105c. yellowtail coris, *Coris gaimard* ♂, hīnālea-ʻaki-lolo, 18.0 in. (457 mm)

106a. cigar wrasse, *Cheilio inermis* ♀, kūpoupou, 12.3 in. (312 mm)

106b. cigar wrasse, *Cheilio inermis* ♂, kūpoupou, 10.6 in. (269 mm)

107a. pearl wrasse, *Anampses cuvier*, 'ōpule, 7.7 in. (196 mm)

107b. pearl wrasse, *Anampses cuvier*, ♂, 'ōpule, 12.2 in. (310 mm)

108a. psychedelic wrasse, *Anampses chrysocephalus* ♀, 2.9 in. (74 mm)

108b. psychedelic wrasse, *Anampses chrysocephalus* ♂, 6.3 in. (160 mm)

109a. saddle wrasse, *Thalassoma duperrey* juv., hīnālea lau-wili, 2.1 in. (53 mm)

109b. saddle wrasse, *Thalassoma duperrey* ♂, hīnālea lau-wili, 2.1 in. (53 mm)

110a. blacktail wrasse, *Thalassoma ballieui* juv., hīnālea luahine, 1.7 in. (43 mm)

110b. blacktail wrasse, *Thalassoma ballieui* ♂, hīnālea luahine, 7.0 in. (178 mm)

111a. **Christmas wrasse,** *Thalassoma trilobatum* ♀, āwela, 7.2 in. (183 mm)

111b. **Christmas wrasse,** *Thalassoma trilobatum* ♂, āwela, 8.0 in. (203 mm)

112. **surge wrasse,** *Thalassoma purpureum* ♂, hou, 15.1 in. (384 mm)

113. **ornate wrasse,** *Halichoeres ornatissimus,* ʻōhua, 4.2 in. (107 mm)

114a. shortnose wrasse, *Macropharyngodon geoffroy* ♀, 2.7 in. (69 mm)

114b. shortnose wrasse, *Macropharyngodon geoffroy* ♂, 5.5 in. (140 mm)

115a. smalltail wrasse, *Pseudojuloides cerasinus* ♀, 3.6 in. (91 mm)

115b. smalltail wrasse, *Pseudojuloides cerasinus* ♂, 3.8 in. (97 mm)

116a. bird wrasse, *Gomphosus varius* ♀, 'aki-lolo, 4.2 in. (107 mm)

116b. bird wrasse, *Gomphosus varius* ♂, hīnālea 'i'iwi, 9.0 in. (229 mm)

117a. belted wrasse, *Stethojulis balteata* ♀, 'ōmaka, 3.9 in. (99 mm)

117b. belted wrasse, *Stethojulis balteata* ♂, 'ōmaka, 4.7 in. (119 mm)

118a. **stareye parrotfish,** *Calotomus carolinus,* pōnuhunuhu, 11.2 in. (284 mm)

118b. **stareye parrotfish,** *Calotomus carolinus,* pōnuhunuhu, 15.4 in. (391 mm)

119a. **yellowbar parrotfish,** *Calotomus zonarchus* ♀, 9.1 in. (231 mm)

119b. **yellowbar parrotfish,** *Calotomus zonarchus* ♂, 9.4 in. (239 mm)

120a. bullethead parrotfish, *Scarus sordidus* ♀, uhu, 7.4 in. (188 mm)

120b. bullethead parrotfish, *Scarus sordidus* ♂, uhu, 10.5 in. (267 mm)

121a. spectacled parrotfish, *Scarus perspicillatus* ♀, uhu ʻahuʻula, 16.0 in. (406 mm)

121b. spectacled parrotfish, *Scarus perspicillatus* ♂, uhu-uliuli, 17.0 in. (432 mm)

122a. palenose parrotfish, *Scarus psittacus* ♀, uhu, 7.4 in. (188 mm)

122b. palenose parrotfish, *Scarus psittacus* ♂, uhu, 7.6 in. (193 mm)

123a. redlip parrotfish, *Scarus rubroviolaceus* ♀, pālukaluka, 20.5 in. (521 mm)

123b. redlip parrotfish, *Scarus rubroviolaceus* ♂, pālukaluka, 18.2 in. (462 mm)

124a. regal parrotfish, *Scarus dubius* ♀, lauia, 10.2 in. (259 mm)

124b. regal parrotfish, *Scarus dubius* ♂, lauia, 10.3 in. (262 mm)

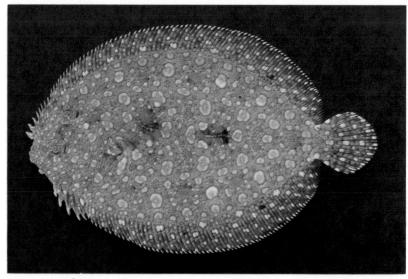

125. manyray flatfish, *Bothus mancus*, pāki'i, 5.0 in. (127 mm)

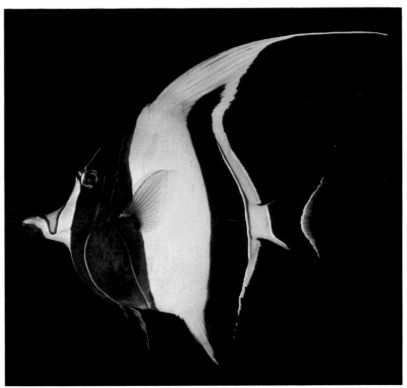

126. moorish idol, *Zanclus cornutus,* kihikihi, 6.8 in. (173 mm)

127. whitespotted surgeonfish, *Acanthurus guttatus,* 'api, 8.0 in. (203 mm)

128. convict tang, *Acanthurus triostegus*, manini, 5.6 in. (142 mm)

129. whitebar surgeonfish, *Acanthurus leucopareius*, māikoiko, 8.4 in. (213 mm)

130. orangeband surgeonfish, *Acanthurus olivaceus*, naʻenaʻe, 6.7 in. (170 mm)

131. eye-stripe surgeonfish, *Acanthurus dussumieri,* palani, 11.2 in. (284 mm)

132. ringtail surgeonfish, *Acanthurus blochii,* pualu, 8.5 in. (216 mm)

133. yellowfin surgeonfish, *Acanthurus xanthopterus,* pualu, 21.5 in. (546 mm)

134. achilles tang, *Acanthurus achilles,* pāku'iku'i, 9.0 in. (229 mm)

135. whitecheek surgeonfish, *Acanthurus glaucopareius,* 8.2 in. (208 mm)

136. brown surgeonfish, *Acanthurus nigrofuscus,* mā'i'i'i, 5.0 in. (127 mm)

137. bluelined surgeonfish, *Acanthurus nigroris*, maiko, 6.4 in. (163 mm)

138. goldring surgeonfish, *Ctenochaetus strigosus*, kole, 4.2 in. (107 mm)

139. black surgeonfish, *Ctenochaetus hawaiiensis*, 10.5 in. (267 mm)

140. **yellow tang,** *Zebrasoma flavescens,* lau'ī-pala, 4.2 in. (107 mm)

141. **sailfin tang,** *Zebrasoma veliferum,* māne'one'o, 5.7 in. (145 mm)

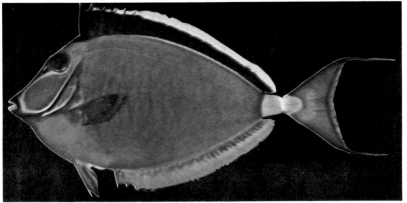

142. orangespine unicornfish, *Naso lituratus*, umaumalei, 8.3 in. (211 mm)

143. bluespine unicornfish, *Naso unicornis*, kala, 18.7 in. (475 mm)

144. sleek unicornfish, *Naso hexacanthus*, kala holo, 13.0 in. (330 mm)

145. spotted unicornfish, *Naso brevirostris*, kala lōlō, 15.0 in. (381 mm)

146. bluespotted goby, *Asterropteryx semipunctatus*, 'o'opu, 2.0 in. (51 mm)

147. noble goby, *Priolepis eugenius*, 'o'opu, 2.2 in. (56 mm)

148. indigo hover goby, *Ptereleotris heteropterus*, 4.7 in. (119 mm)

149. marbled blenny, *Entomacrodus marmoratus*, pāo'o, 4.6 in. (117 mm)

150. zebra blenny, *Istiblennius zebra*, pāo'o, 3.2 in. (81 mm)

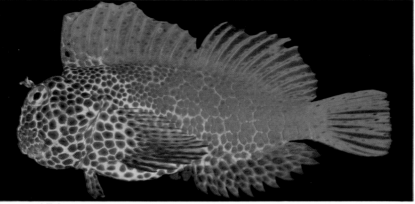

151. shortbodied blenny, *Exallias brevis,* pāoʻo kauila, 4.6 in. (117 mm)

152. scarface blenny, *Cirripectes vanderbilti,* 3.7 in. (94 mm)

153. gargantuan blenny, *Cirripectes obscurus,* 6.9 in. (175 mm)

154. Ewa blenny, *Plagiotremus ewaensis,* 2.3 in. (58 mm)

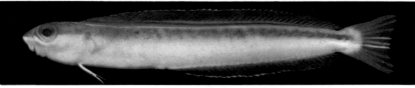

155. scale-eating blenny, *Plagiotremus goslinei,* 2.0 in. (51 mm)

156. squaretail filefish, *Cantherhines sandwichiensis*, ʻōʻili-lepa, 6.6 in. (168 mm)

157. barred filefish, *Cantherhines dumerilii*, ʻōʻili, 12.5 in. (317 mm)

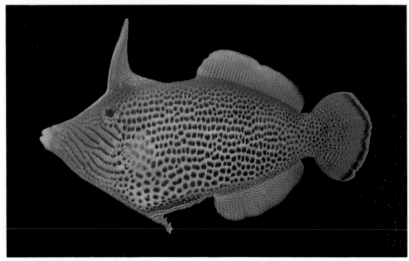

158. fantail filefish, *Pervagor spilosoma*, ʻōʻili-ʻuwīʻuwī, 5.3 in. (135 mm)

159. **lacefin filefish,** *Pervagor aspricaudus,* 3.2 in. (81 mm)

160. **reef triggerfish,** *Rhinecanthus rectangulus,* humuhumu-nukunuku-a-pua'a, 6.6 in. (168 mm)

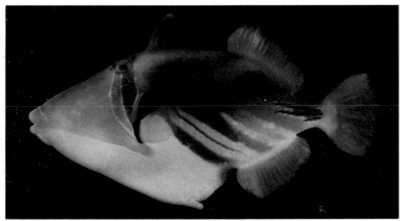

161. **lagoon triggerfish,** *Rhinecanthus aculeatus,* humuhumu-nukunuku-a-pua'a, 7.4 in. (188 mm)

162a. gilded triggerfish, *Xanthichthys auromarginatus* ♀, 6.3 in. (160 mm)

162b. gilded triggerfish, *Xanthichthys auromarginatus* ♂, 5.7 in. (145 mm)

163. lei triggerfish, *Sufflamen bursa*, humuhumu lei, 5.7 in. (145 mm)

164. bridled triggerfish, *Sufflamen fraenatus,* humuhumu-mimi, 10.0 in. (254 mm)

165. pinktail durgon, *Melichthys vidua,* humuhumu-hi'u-kole, 8.1 in. (206 mm)

166. black durgon, *Melichthys niger,* humuhumu-'ele'ele, 6.2 in. (157 mm)

167a. spotted trunkfish, *Ostracion meleagris* ♀, moa, 3.6 in. (91 mm)

167b. spotted trunkfish, *Ostracion meleagris* ♂, moa, 5.1 in. (130 mm)

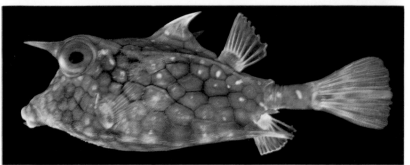

168. thornback cowfish, *Lactoria fornasini*, makukana, 3.0 in. (76 mm)

169. Ambon toby, *Canthigaster amboinensis*, 2.7 in. (69 mm)

170. Hawaiian whitespotted toby, *Canthigaster jactator*, 3.1 in. (79 mm)

171. crown toby, *Canthigaster coronata*, 3.7 in. (94 mm)

172. lantern toby, *Canthigaster epilampra*, 3.3 in. (84 mm)

173. maze toby, *Canthigaster rivulata*, 6.2 in. (157 mm)

174. stripebelly puffer, *Arothron hispidus,* keke, 11.0 in. (279 mm)

175. spotted puffer, *Arothron meleagris,* ʻoʻopu-hue, 9.8 in. (249 mm)

176. porcupinefish, *Diodon hystrix,* kōkala, 13.5 in. (343 mm)

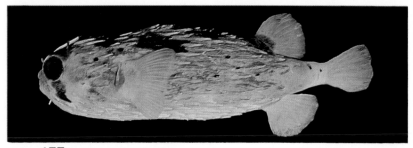

177. spiny puffer, *Diodon holocanthus.* ʻoʻopu okala, 10.0 in. (254 mm)

87. *Stegastes fasciolatus* (Ogilby), **1889.**   **Pacific gregory**
Dorsal rays XIII,15 to 17; anal rays II,12 or 13 (usually 13); pectoral rays 20 or 21; tubed lateral-line scales 20; depth of body 1.8 to 2.05 in standard length; dorsal profile of head convex; maxilla reaching to or beyond a vertical at front edge of eye; teeth in one row, slender, close-set, with truncate (or slightly bifid) tips; posterior margin of preopercle serrate. Brownish gray, often with dark blotches, the edges of the scales dark brown, giving an effect of near-vertical dark lines on body; caudal, anal, and posterior dorsal fins dark brown; rest of dorsal fin brown except outer part of first three interspinous membranes which is black; pectoral fins pale with a small black spot at upper base; iris yellow. Reaches about 5 inches in the Hawaiian Islands where it is one of the most abundant of shallow-water reef fishes. Indo Pacific. Avoids the zone of heavy surge and high tidepools. Feeds mainly on filamentous algae and detritus. Matures at about 3.5 inches; reported to spawn from December to March. The Bishop Museum has night-light collections of ¾-inch young taken in May and June. *Pomacentrus jenkinsi* Jordan and Evermann is a synonym.

88. *Dascyllus albisella* Gill, **1862.**   **Hawaiian dascyllus, 'ālo'ilo'i**
Dorsal rays XII,14 to 16 (usually 16); anal rays II,14 or 15; pectoral rays 19 to 21; tubed lateral-line scales 18 to 20; deep-bodied, the depth 1.5 to 1.65 in standard length; body oval, the anterior profile nearly semicircular; teeth in 4 or 5 irregular rows at front of jaws, the outer row of blunt canines, the inner rows progressively smaller; margins of suborbital, subopercle and both limbs of preopercle finely serrate; caudal fin slightly emarginate to truncate with rounded corners; two small free spines at base of caudal fin at upper and lower edges. Blackish, the centers of the scales whitish; a large whitish spot straddling lateral line below base of ninth dorsal spine. Juveniles are blacker, the spot on the side relatively larger and whiter; also a median pale blue spot on nape. To 5 inches. Hawaiian Islands. Very close to *D. trimaculatus* (Rüppell) from elsewhere in the Indo-Pacific; some authors might regard *D. albisella* as only a subspecies of *D. trimaculatus.* Occurs from very shallow (but protected) water to about 150 feet. The young often take shelter among the branches of coral (*Pocillopora*), occasionally commensal with the sand-dwelling anemone *Marcanthia cookei.* Feeds on mysids, shrimp and crab larvae, copepods, pelagic tunicates, and other elements of the zooplankton, sometimes as much as 20 feet above the bottom. Maximum spawning May to August. Nuptial coloration of males white except black caudal and anal fins and margin of dorsal fin. Eggs almost colorless, averaging 0.85 mm in length. Newly transformed juveniles average 15 mm (0.6 inches). Growth of juveniles 5.1 mm (0.2 inches) per month. It is estimated that sexual maturity is attained in one year. In Australia the species of *Dascyllus* are called humbugs.

89. *Chromis hanui* Randall and Swerdloff, **1973.**   **chocolate-dip chromis**
Dorsal rays XII,13; anal rays II,12 to 14; pectoral rays 17 or 18; tubed lateral-line scales 15 to 18; depth of body 1.85 to 1.95 in standard length. Close to *C. agilis,* differing in suborbital margin free only to about anterior edge of eye, and in color. Dark yellowish brown, the caudal peduncle and fin abruptly white slightly posterior to rear base of dorsal and anal fins; a large black spot at pectoral base; no pink on head or chest. Reaches 3.5 inches. Restricted to the Hawaiian Islands. Has been collected at depths of 6 to 165 feet. *C. hanui* has also been confused with *C. leucura* Gilbert, another dark brown species with a white caudal fin. *C. leucura* is known from only a few specimens taken in 100 feet or more; it has 14 dorsal rays, 16 pectoral rays, a yellow zone on pectoral base behind the black basal spot, and yellow instead of brown pelvic fins.

90. *Chromis agilis* Smith, 1950.   **agile chromis**
Dorsal rays XII,12 to 14; anal rays II,12 to 14; pectoral rays 17 or 18; tubed lateral-line scales 15 to 17; depth of body 1.7 to 2 in standard length; conical teeth typical of the genus; lower suborbital margin free to beneath center of eye; second branched caudal ray of each lobe extended as a filament. Orange-brown, suffused with lavender or pink over lower head and chest; caudal fin and posterior half of caudal peduncle whitish; a large black spot at base of pectoral fin. Largest specimen, 4.4 inches. Indo-Pacific, in about 15 to 200 feet. A common species in Hawaii; it seems to be more abundant on the lee side of the islands. Also known as the reef chromis.

91. *Chromis ovalis* (Steindachner), 1900.   **oval chromis**
Dorsal rays XIV,11 to 13; anal rays II,12 or 13 (usually 13); pectoral rays 20 to 22; tubed lateral-line scales 19 to 21; depth of body 2 to 2.35 in standard length; short conical teeth in jaws with one or two irregular inner rows of small teeth (only anteriorly on lower jaw); preopercular margin smooth; two short spines on upper and lower caudal base. Bluish to greenish, the edges of scales yellowish brown, shading to silvery gray ventrally; pectoral fins with black spot on upper half of base. Juveniles blue with a yellow band at base of dorsal fin. Largest specimen, 7.6 inches. Hawaiian Islands; collected from the depth range of 20 to 150 feet. Feeds on copepods (about 60% by volume), pelagic tunicates (17%), mysids, euphausids, crustacean larvae, larval polychaetes, siphonophores, and fish eggs. Attains maturity at about 5 inches; spawning occurs from February through May. The eggs are transparent, 0.6 mm long; larvae hatch in 72 hours at an average length of 2.4 mm.

92. *Chromis verater* Jordan and Metz, 1912.   **threespot chromis**
Dorsal rays XIV,12 to 14; anal rays II,12 to 14; pectoral rays 19 or 20; tubed lateral-line scales 17 to 19; depth of body 1.8 to 2.1 in standard length; dentition similar to *C. ovalis*; preopercular margin smooth; three short spines on upper and lower caudal fin base. Blackish with three white spots about the size of pupil, one at rear base of dorsal fin, one at rear base of anal fin, and the third at mid-base of caudal fin (these spots sometimes faint); a large nearly triangular black spot at upper base of pectoral fin. Attains 8.5 inches. Known only from the Hawaiian Islands. Not common in less than about 60 feet, but abundant in deeper water. Reported from submarine observations off western Oahu to be the dominant species of fish at outcrops of reef rock in 230 feet. Has been collected in 600 feet. Feeds on a wide variety of animals of the plankton, particularly copepods (about 70% of the diet). Spawning occurs from December to June. The eggs average 0.65 mm in length. The larvae seem indistinguishable in morphology from those of *C. ovalis* and have the same developmental rate.

93. *Chromis vanderbilti* (Fowler), 1941.   **blackfin chromis**
Dorsal rays XII,11; anal rays II,11; pectoral rays 16 to 18; tubed lateral-line scales 16 to 18; body elongate, the depth 2.3 to 2.65 in standard length; dentition as in the preceding species of *Chromis*; preopercle smooth. Side of body yellow with blue stripes; anal fin black except region of last few rays; lower edge of caudal fin broadly black. Largest specimen, 2.8 inches. Oceania. Common in Hawaii in about 15 to 50 feet. Often observed in aggregations. Feeds on zooplankton, especially copepods. The related *C. acares* Randall and Swerdloff, known in the Hawaiian area only from Johnston Island, is also small with a black anal fin; it is mainly blue with a yellow spot at the rear base of the dorsal fin; the caudal fin has a broad yellow band on each lobe.

WRASSES (LABRIDAE)

Forty-two species of wrasses occur in Hawaii, making them the largest family in the islands. These fishes are very diverse in size and form. Typically, they have thick lips and protruding teeth; there are no teeth on the roof of the mouth but there are strong nodular teeth on the pharyngeal bones in the gill region which many of these fishes use to crush mollusks, crabs, sea urchins, and other invertebrates with hard parts. The scales are cycloid. There is a single dorsal fin with VIII to XIV spines; usually there are III anal spines. Most species are brightly and often complexly colored. Juveniles frequently have a different pattern from adults, and the sexes of many wrasses are so disparate in color that some have been described as different species. Sex reversal has been demonstrated for several species and appears to be general for the family. These fishes commence their adult life as females and later may alter their sex to males, usually assuming a gaudier color pattern referred to as the terminal phase. For some species there are both mature males and females in the initial color phase. These tend to spawn in aggregations whereas terminal males reproduce with single females. Wrasses are carnivorous and diurnal. They are among the first fishes to retire to an inactive state on the bottom with the approach of darkness and among the last to resume activity the following morning. Each species appears to enter and leave a state of torpor on the cue of a specific low light level. Most of the smaller species bury in the sand at night. When speaking of wrasses in general, the Hawaiian name hīnālea is most often applied to the family. Of the 17 wrasses for which there are no species accounts herein, six are razorfishes [Cymolutes lecluse (Quoy and Gaimard) and Xyrichtys spp.] which live over stretches of open sand and dive into the sediment with the approach of danger; two appear to be restricted to the Leeward Hawaiian Islands [the slingjaw wrasse Epibulus insidiator (Pallas) and Bodianus vulpinus (Richardson), of which B. oxycephalus (Bleeker) is a synonym]; three are common Indo-Pacific species which are rare in Hawaii [Thalassoma lutescens (Lay and Bennett), T. quinquevittatum (Lay and Bennett), and Halichoeres marginatus Rüppell], the last known from only a single specimen]; five are deep-water species [Bodianus sanguineus (Jordan and Evermann), Bodianus cylindriatus (Tanaka), Polylepion russelli (Gomon and Randall), Suezichthys notatus (Kamohara), and Novaculichthys woodi Jenkins]; and two are small cryptic forms which are rarely seen (Pseudocheilinus evanidus Jordan and Evermann and Wetmorella albofasciata Schultz and Marshall).

94. *Novaculichthys taeniourus* (Lacepède), 1801.   **rockmover**

Dorsal rays IX,12; anal rays III,12; pectoral rays 13; lateral-line interrupted, 19 or 20 pored scales on upper anterior portion and 4 or 5 on caudal peduncle; body moderately deep, the depth 2.65 to 3 in standard length, and compressed, the width 2.4 to 3 in depth; head naked except for two scales on upper opercle and a near-vertical row of small scales behind eye; a pair of large curved canine teeth at front of jaws; first two dorsal spines flexible, greatly elongate on juveniles; caudal fin rounded. Dark brown with a vertical white line on each scale; usually reddish over abdomen; a blue-edged arc of black behind base of pectoral fin, largely covered by fin; a black spot on first dorsal membrane and another on second; a broad white band at caudal fin base. Young are green to brown with white blotches, dark bands radiating from eye, and clear areas in dorsal fin. Reaches about 1 foot. Indo-Pacific. Generally found over sand and rubble near reefs. Feeds on pelecypods, gastropods, sea urchins, brittle stars, polychaete worms, and crabs. Has been observed to move stones with its jaws in search of invertebrates beneath. The young mimic drifting masses of algae. *N. bifer* (Lay and Bennett) is a synonym, based on the juvenile form.

95. *Cheilinus unifasciatus* Streets, 1877. ringtail wrasse, pō'ou

Dorsal rays IX,10; anal rays III,8; pectoral rays 12; lateral line interrupted, the pored scales in upper anterior series 15 or 16 and those in peduncular row 6 to 8; depth of body 2.55 to 3.2 in standard length; head scaled except snout, anterior interorbital and a broad marginal zone of preopercle; preopercular margin smooth; lower jaw projecting; anterior pair of canines three or more times larger than remaining teeth in jaws; caudal fin rounded. Olive green, the base of each body scale with a dull orange bar; a white or pinkish white bar at front of caudal peduncle; head with orange bands radiating from eye and diagonally across cheek. Largest specimen examined, 18 inches (3.1 pounds). Tropical Pacific. Not uncommon in Hawaii where it has been collected in the depth range of 30 to 528 feet. The stomachs of 33 adults were opened; 23 contained food, of which 65% by volume was fishes (among them a surgeonfish and a filefish); the remaining material consisted of crabs (13%), brittle stars (13%), heart urchins and sea urchins. Two fully ripe females collected in March were only 8 inches long. A few of these fish in Hawaii have been reported to cause fish poisoning (ciguatera) when eaten. Often misidentified as *Cheilinus rhodochrous* Playfair and Günther.

96. *Cheilinus bimaculatus* Cuvier and Valenciennes, 1839. twospot wrasse

Dorsal rays IX,10; anal rays III,8; pectoral rays 12 (rarely 13); lateral line interrupted, the pored scales in upper anterior series 15 or 16, those in mid-lateral row on caudal peduncle 6 or 7; depth of body 2.6 to 3.1 in standard length; head scaled except snout (and chin) and anterior interorbital space; preopercular margin smooth; lower jaw slightly projecting; a pair of large slightly incurved canine teeth at front of jaws, the lower pair medial to the upper, followed by a row of smaller conical teeth along sides of jaws; caudal fin rounded in females, rhomboid with the upper rays produced as a pointed lobe in males. Brown to reddish brown (the males may have a greenish cast), blotched and finely flecked with whitish; a dark green spot behind eye and a black spot on upper side between pectoral tip and lateral line (on sixth vertical scale row); narrow orange bands radiating from eye; a small dark green spot partially rimmed with red on first interspinous membrane of dorsal fin. A small species, probably not exceeding 6 inches. Indo-Pacific. Not common in less than about 50 feet, but becoming abundant in 100 feet or more; deepest Hawaiian collection 335 feet, from a trawl. Seen more often on rubble or rubble-sand bottoms than on well developed coral reefs.

97. *Labroides phthirophagus* Randall, 1958. Hawaiian cleaner wrasse

Dorsal rays IX,11; anal rays III,10; pectoral rays 13; lateral-line scales 27; depth of body 3.5 to 3.7 in standard length; head scaleless; lower lip divided into two prominent anterior-projecting lobes; a pair of curved canine teeth anteriorly in jaws and a single canine at corner of mouth; preopercular margin smooth; caudal fin slightly rounded. Yellow with a median dorsal black band on head and mid-lateral black stripe which passes through eye and expands in mid-body to nearly full body width except for upper and lower edges of caudal peduncle which are magenta, this color continuing broadly onto upper and lower caudal fin margins; dorsal and anal fins blue, the spinous portion of dorsal blackish basally. Males and females appear identical in color. Juveniles are black with a broad band of purple on back. Largest specimen, 4 inches. Hawaiian Islands. Known from depth range of 2 to 300 feet. Establishes cleaning stations on reefs to which resident fishes come for removal of crustacean ectoparasites. In the process the cleaning wrasse also feeds on mucus and not infrequently ingests some scales from the host fishes. Reproduction is year-around. Spawning occurs in pairs, preceded by courtship. The spawning run consists of a very rapid dash, generally upward, for about 18 inches, with the release of eggs and sperm by the contiguous fish at the peak of the movement. This fish does not bury in the sand at night like nearly all small wrasses; while inactive on the bottom at night a cocoon of mucus accumulates around it similar to that observed for many of the parrotfishes.

98. *Pseudocheilinus octotaenia* **Jenkins, 1900.**   **eightline wrasse**
Dorsal rays IX,11; anal rays III,9; pectoral rays 14; lateral line interrupted, the upper anterior pored scales 17 or 18 and the peduncular series 6 or 7; depth of body 2.9 to 3.4 in standard length; snout pointed, moderately long, 2.6 to 2.95 in head; preopercular margin membranous; head scaled except ventrally, on snout, and interorbital; a curious double pupil from a division of the cornea of eye; three large canine teeth on each side at front of upper jaw, the third notably the largest and sharply curved outward and posteriorly; lower jaw with one pair of large canines anteriorly which fit between the first and second pair of large upper teeth when mouth is closed; an inner row of small teeth anteriorly which continues as a single row along sides of jaws; caudal fin rounded. Orangish with eight narrow dark purple to dark brown stripes on body following scale rows; cheek purplish with yellow spots; median fins yellow with purple bands or small spots. Largest specimen, 5.2 inches. Indo-Pacific. Reported from as little as 5 feet; deepest Bishop Museum collection, 135 feet. Somewhat cryptic in habits, thus more common than underwater observations would indicate. Small benthic crustaceans predominate in the diet, followed by mollusks and echinoids. Planktonic animals such as crab megalops are eaten if they come close to the bottom.

99. *Pseudocheilinus tetrataenia* **Schultz, 1960.**   **fourline wrasse**
Dorsal rays IX,11 (rarely 12); anal rays III,9; pectoral rays 16 (rarely 17); lateral line interrupted, the upper anterior series of pored scales 17 or 18 and the peduncular series 5 to 7; depth of body 2.7 to 3.2 in standard length; snout moderately long and somewhat produced, 2.9 to 3.05 in head; preopercular margin membranous, the upper edge scaled over; head squamation, pupil structure, and dentition similar to *P. octotaenia* but with four pairs of canines at front of upper jaw, the fourth pair twice as long as the first three and strongly curved; first two dorsal spines with long filaments. Terracotta with four narrow dark-edged blue stripes on upper half of body and a narrow fifth one on nape; lower part of head and chest whitish, separated from reddish color of rest of head and pectoral region by a band of light blue; a broad violet band at base of anal fin and two narrow violet bands in dorsal fin; pelvic fins violet. Largest specimen, 2.7 inches. Islands of Oceania. Bishop Museum specimens have been taken in the depth range of 20 to 145 feet. A secretive species; not uncommon but rarely seen. A third species of the genus in the Hawaiian Islands, *P. evanidus* Jordan and Evermann, is red with narrow whitish longitudinal lines on the body and a broad white to light blue streak on the cheek.

100. *Cirrhilabrus jordani* **Snyder, 1904.**   **flame wrasse**
Dorsal rays XI,9; anal rays III,9; pectoral rays 15; lateral line interrupted, 17 pored scales on upper anterior portion and 5 or 6 on peduncular part; depth of body 3 to 3.45 in standard length; upper preopercular margin finely serrate (smooth on the remaining species of Labridae herein); head scaled except ventrally, on snout, and interorbital space; three large canine teeth on each side at front of upper jaw, the lateral two outcurved, and one on each side at front of lower jaw; an inner row of small sharp teeth continuing as a single row on side of jaws; a double pupil as in *Pseudocheilinus*; caudal fin rounded. Females red, the lower head yellowish; median fins yellowish; males deeper red, suffused with yellow on sides, becoming deep yellow ventrally; a curved red band from chin under eye to edge of gill cover; dorsal and caudal fins deep red; anal and pelvic fins yellow. Largest Bishop Museum specimen, 4 inches. Hawaiian Islands; rare in less than 60 feet. Feeds on zooplankton; usually seen in small aggregations.

101. *Bodianus bilunulatus* (Lacepède), 1801.   Hawaiian hogfish, 'a'awa
Dorsal rays XII,10; anal rays III,12; pectoral rays 15 to 17; lateral line complete, with 31 or 32 pored scales; depth of body 2.6 to 3 in standard length; head scaled except ventrally and on snout; preopercular margin finely serrate in juveniles, smooth in adults; caudal fin truncate in young and double emarginate in adults with lobes prolonged. Females white anteriorly, grading to light yellow posteriorly, with longitudinal brown lines which shade to yellow as they pass backward on body; a dark band from snout through lower eye to edge of gill cover with a broad white zone beneath; a large black spot under posterior part of dorsal fin and adjacent caudal peduncle; anal, caudal, and posterior dorsal fins yellow; a black spot at front of dorsal fin. Males are wine-colored to purplish brown, the black spot below rear of dorsal fin often faint or absent. Juveniles are whitish with reddish brown lines anteriorly, becoming broadly black posteriorly on body and dorsal and anal fins, then abruptly white on posterior caudal peduncle and fin; upper head, nape, and most of spinous portion of dorsal fin abruptly yellow. Largest specimen examined, 20 inches. The author has collected specimens from 25 to 110 feet; submarine observations to 360 feet. There are three populations of this species: Hawaii, southeast Oceania, and the western Pacific and Indian Oceans. The Hawaiian form was described as a species, *albotaeniatus* (Cuvier and Valenciennes) in 1839, a name perhaps best retained as a subspecies. The gut contents of 50 specimens revealed heavy feeding on mollusks (about equally on gastropods and pelecypods), sea urchins, hermit crabs, and crabs; brittle stars and small fishes are occasionally taken. Ripe fish have been noted from December to February. Two other species of *Bodianus* and the related monotypic genus *Polylepion* occur in the Hawaiian Islands in relatively deep water.

102. *Coris ballieui* Vaillant and Sauvage, 1875.   lined coris, malamalama
Dorsal rays IX,12; anal rays III,12 (rarely 11); pectoral rays 13; lateral line complete on this and other species of *Coris,* the pored scales 51 to 53; depth of body 3.05 to 3.8 in standard length; head scaleless; preopercular margin smooth (true of other *Coris*); first and second dorsal spines with tips flexible, longer than third spine (the first spine of males as long or longer than head); space between first two dorsal spines narrower than remaining interdorsal spaces; anterior pair of canine teeth nearly twice as long as second canines. Initial phase (mainly female) yellowish white with longitudinal lines of rose to salmon along centers of scales (color deeper dorsally); median fins yellowish with faint blue bands. Terminal males yellowish with narrow blue stripes or rows of spots except area of upper abdomen, where blue markings are irregular (mainly vertical), and upper anterior part of body which is deeper yellow (or even pink) with blue markings reduced or absent, often with a broad dusky bar; dark-edged blue bands on head and median fins; a black spot basally on first interspinous dorsal fin membrane. Largest specimen, 12 inches. Hawaiian Islands. Rare in less than 60 feet. Deepest collection, 265 feet, but probably ranges into much deeper water. *C. rosea* Vaillant and Sauvage, named for the initial phase, is a synonym.

103. *Coris venusta* Vaillant and Sauvage, 1875.   elegant coris
Dorsal rays IX,12; anal rays III,12; pectoral rays 13; lateral line complete, pored scales 50 or 51; depth of body 3.4 to 3.8 in standard length; head scaleless; first and second dorsal spines sharp-tipped, shorter than third; dorsal spines nearly equally spaced; anterior canine teeth only slightly larger than second canines. Red bands on head extending onto anterior third of body; posterior two-thirds with numerous narrow diagonal red bars on lower side; a black spot on opercular flap edged posteriorly with yellow; a small black spot often present at rear base of dorsal fin. Largest specimen, 7.6 inches. Hawaiian Islands; a common shallow-water reef fish. Stomach contents of 15 adults consisted of pelecypods

(37.5%), gastropods (32%), crabs, sea urchins, heart urchins, hermit crabs, shrimps, polychaetes, amphipods, isopods, chitons, and foraminifera.

104. *Coris flavovittata* (Bennett), 1829.   yellowstripe coris, hilu
Dorsal rays IX,12; anal rays III,12; pectoral rays 14; lateral-line scales small, 75 to 83; depth of body varying from 2.7 in standard length of large adults to 4.2 in standard length of juveniles; head scaleless; first two dorsal spines flexible, longer and more closely spaced than more posterior spines (except juveniles); front pair of canine teeth nearly twice as long as second canines. Initial phase dark brown dorsally with two yellow stripes, light red shading to whitish ventrally, with a mid-lateral yellowish white stripe; median fins mainly dark brown with pale blue margins, the dorsal with a row of yellow spots and an ocellated black spot at the front; a blue spot on opercular flap. Terminal phase greenish dorsally becoming yellowish on lower side with dark reticular markings (often interrupted with a large pink area centered between soft portions of dorsal and anal fins); head, chest, and ventral part of body light bluish with indistinct irregular pale reddish spots; a blue and black spot on opercular flap. Juveniles are dark brown with five narrow light yellow stripes. Reaches 20 inches. Hawaiian Islands. Gut contents of 15 adults consisted of sea urchins and heart urchins (31.8%), pelecypods (23.4%), gastropods (22.6%), brittle stars (15.5%), crabs, hermit crabs, and polychaetes. The scientific name is based on the juvenile form; *C. eydouxii* (Cuvier and Valenciennes) (initial phase) and *C. lepomis* (Jenkins) (terminal male) are synonyms.

105. *Coris gaimard* (Quoy and Gaimard), 1824.   yellowtail coris, hīnālea-'aki-lolo
Dorsal rays IX,12; anal rays III,12; pectoral rays 13; lateral-line scales 70 to 79; depth of body 3.3 to 3.7 in standard length; head scaleless; first two dorsal spines flexible, notably longer than third spine (except small juveniles), the space between them narrower than the spaces between more posterior spines; front canine teeth nearly twice as large as second canines. Ruddy to dark greenish with small brilliant blue spots which are more numerous posteriorly; head brownish orange with green bands; caudal fin bright yellow. Terminal males develop a green bar on side of body at level of origin of anal fin, a broad dark band, edged with blue in outer part of dorsal and anal fins and more numerous small blue spots. Juveniles are red with three large black-edged white spots dorsally on body which extend into dorsal fin and two similar but smaller spots on upper head. Attains about 15 inches. Indo-Pacific. Feeds mainly on mollusks, crabs, and hermit crabs. *C. greenovii* (Bennett), named for the juvenile stage, is a synonym.

106. *Cheilio inermis* (Forsskål), 1775.   cigar wrasse, kūpoupou
Dorsal rays IX,12 or 13; anal rays III,11 or 12; pectoral rays 12 or 13; lateral line complete, the pored scales 45 to 47; body very elongate, the depth 5.5 to 7.8 in standard length; head naked except for a few scales behind eye on preopercle and opercle; width of body about 1.7 in depth; snout long, 2.2 to 2.4 in head. Color variable; may be olive green, brown, orange-brown, or yellow; a narrow mid-lateral black streak or row of spots on body of many individuals. Large males appear to lack this stripe; instead they have a large pale pink area on upper side at end of pectoral fin containing a few small dark brown spots. Reaches about 20 inches. Indo-Pacific, in shallow water. Although found on coral reefs it is more common on open bottoms with rich plant growth in which it is a master at hiding and evasive movement. Feeds on gastropods, pelecypods, hermit crabs, crabs, sea urchins, and shrimps.

107. *Anampses cuvier* Quoy and Gaimard, 1824.   pearl wrasse, 'ōpule
Dorsal rays IX,12; anal rays III,12; pectoral rays 13; lateral-line scales 27; gill rakers 18 to 21; depth of body 2.35 to 2.7 in standard length; head scaleless; preopercular margin

smooth; a single pair of broad forward-projecting teeth at front of jaws; remaining teeth minute or imperceptible; caudal fin truncate to slightly rounded. Females brown to olive brown, shading to red ventrally, with a bluish white spot on each scale; thorax and lower half of head spotted with red. Males brown on body, each scale with a dark-edged vertical blue line; upper anterior part of head green; rest of head with reticular blue markings. Reaches about 14 inches. Hawaiian Islands. An inshore species of rocky bottom, but may be seen in at least 80 feet. Feeds on a great variety of very small invertebrates, especially crustaceans. *A. godeffroyi* Günther is a synonym, based on the male form.

108. *Anampses chrysocephalus* **Randall, 1958.** **psychedelic wrasse**
Dentition, squamation, and counts the same as *A. cuvier* except for gill rakers, 16 to 18; depth of body 3.25 to 3.95 in standard length; caudal fin rounded. Females dark brown with a white spot on each scale; unscaled part of caudal fin white basally, abruptly red on outer part. Males brown with a faint blue spot on each scale, the head bright orange with dark-edged blue spots and a mid-dorsal yellow spot on nape; a black spot on opercular flap. Attains 7 inches. Hawaiian Islands. Generally observed at depths greater than 50 feet. The most important wrasse in the Hawaiian aquarium fish trade (eighth in total catch). *A. rubrocaudatus* Randall is a synonym, named for the red-tailed female form.

109. *Thalassoma duperrey* **(Quoy and Gaimard), 1824.**
saddle wrasse, hīnālea lau-wili
Dorsal rays VIII,12; anal rays III,11; pectoral rays 16 (rarely 15 or 17); lateral-line scales 26; gill rakers 20 to 23; depth of body 2.8 to 3.4 in standard length; head scaleless; anterior canine teeth the largest; no canine at corner of mouth; free margin of preopercle a short curved vertical at level of mouth; pelvic fins not reaching anus; caudal fin varies from slightly rounded in juveniles to lunate in large males. Body green with a vertical red line on each scale except for a broad anterior zone of solid orange (demarcation at base of third dorsal spine; zone includes anterior abdomen, chest, and nape); head purplish blue; a black spot on second dorsal interspinous membrane (sometimes also on first and third membranes) and one at upper base of pectoral fins; a red band in upper and another in lower part of caudal fin. Terminal males develop a broad deep blue-black band from middle to top of pectoral fins and a whitish bar on side behind orange anterior collar. Juveniles have a broad black stripe on body at level of upper end of gill opening and lack the orange collar. Reaches about 10 inches. Known only from the Hawaiian Islands where it is the most abundant of inshore reef fishes; occurs from the shallows to at least 70 feet. The stomach contents of 37 specimens indicate a variable diet on small invertebrates; small crustaceans (mostly benthic such as crabs, hermit crabs, shrimps, amphipods, and barnacles but some planktonic such as copepods) (29.4% by volume), pelecypods (21.9%), polychaetes and other worms (17.6%), brittle stars (10.6%), sea urchins and heart urchins (7.9%), and gastropods (7.6%). The remaining stomach contents consisted of tunicates, fish remains, foraminifera, algae (probably ingested incidentally with animal prey), unidentified soft animal tissue and detritus. The author has observed the cleaning of other fishes by juveniles and occasionally by adults as well. Spawning occurs either in aggregations by fish in the initial color phase or in pairs, typically with the terminal male much larger than the female.

110. *Thalassoma ballieui* **(Vaillant and Sauvage), 1875.**
blacktail wrasse, hīnālea luahine
Dorsal rays VIII,13; anal rays III,11; pectoral rays 15 (rarely 14); lateral-line scales 26; gill rakers 24 to 27; depth of body 2.7 to 3.5 in standard length; head scaleless; anterior canine teeth the largest; no tooth at corner of mouth; no lower free margin of preopercle (free margin vertical from corner to slightly above level of mouth); pelvic fins short, not

approaching anus; caudal fin slightly rounded in juveniles to lunate in large adult males. Body brownish gray with vertical maroon lines on scales, shading posteriorly on caudal peduncle and fin to blackish; head light brown with a wash of blue on chin. Unlike other Hawaiian *Thalassoma*, the large male form of *ballieui* is not very different from the initial color phase; the ground color of the body is light greenish yellow and the head dark bluish gray with more blue on the chin (thus the dark head and tail are more in contrast to the lighter body than on smaller fish); also the pectoral fin is dark yellowish blue-green with an outer broad zone of deep blue on upper and middle part. Juveniles are yellowish green. Found only in the Hawaiian Islands. Largest Bishop Museum specimen, 15.5 inches. Stomach contents of 20 adults consisted of sea urchins and heart urchins (23.5%), crabs (23%), fishes (21%), gastropods (9%), lobster, hermit crab and other crustacean remains (7.5%), brittle stars (5%), pelecypods, gastropod eggs, damselfish eggs, and starfish.

111. *Thalassoma trilobatum* (Lacepède), 1801. **Christmas wrasse, 'āwela**
Dorsal rays VIII,13; anal rays III,11; pectoral rays 15 or 16 (usually 16); lateral-line scales 26; gill rakers 18 to 23 (usually 19 to 21); depth 2.9 to 3.3 in standard length; dentition, squamation, preopercle, and pelvic fins as in the preceding two *Thalassoma*; caudal fin varies from slightly rounded in young to emarginate on large males. Body of initial-phase fish rose and green, the green in the form of two longitudinal series of close-set (sometime conjoined) vertical green rectangles, an irregular zone ventrally on body, and five bars linking dorsal fin to upper series of rectangles; rose overlaid with three series of short maroon bars in blocks; head and nape green with irregular maroon spots and short bands; a black spot on first two interspinous membranes of dorsal fin. Terminal males lose the maroon markings, the head becomes uniform orangish brown, the two series of green rectangles are partially blue and the pectoral fins yellow basally, shading through blue to black distally. Largest specimen, 11.6 inches. Indo-Pacific, except the Red Sea and Easter Island. An abundant species of rocky bottom in the surge zone. Feeds primarily on crustaceans (especially crabs), mollusks, and brittle stars. The author has observed spawning both by initial-phase fish of like color in aggregations and by pairs with the large male in terminal color pattern. In both cases the fish made extremely rapid upward rushes, releasing eggs and sperm at the peak of these movements. Often identified as *T. fuscum* Lacepède, but this is a homonym, hence invalid.

112. *Thalassoma purpureum* (Forsskål), 1775. **surge wrasse, hou**
Dorsal rays VIII,13; anal rays III,11; pectoral rays 15 to 17 (nearly always 16); lateral-line scales 26; gill rakers 21 to 25 (usually 22 to 24). Identical in external morphology to *T. trilobatum*, and the initial color phase of both are nearly indistinguishable. The terminal male color phases of these two species, though similar, are easily differentiated; the color of *purpureum*: turquoise to blue-green on head, chest, abdomen, posteriorly on body, and on caudal fin; three irregular pink stripes on body, the upper one broadest, continuing dorsally onto head and snout; a pink band running diagonally from eye toward chest, branching at edge of preopercle. Largest specimen, 16 inches. Indo-Pacific, ranging from the Red Sea to Easter Island. Less common than *T. trilobatum* in the Hawaiian Islands. Lives in very shallow, often turbulent water of wave-swept rocky coasts or reef flats. The stomachs of 19 adults were opened, four of which were empty. The remaining 15 contained by volume: crabs (26%), fish remains (25.2%), sea urchins (18.9%), including one with *Echinometra* and two with slate pencil urchins *(Heterocentrotus)*, pelecypods (7.1%), gastropods (7%), brittle stars (6.6%), polychaete worms (6%), unidentified worms (2%), and unidentified crustaceans (1.2%). Takes a hook readily, thus the larger individuals are rare in areas of intensive shore fishing. *T. umbrostygma*

(Rüppell) is a synonym based on the initial color phase. Two other species of *Thalassoma* occur in Hawaii, but both are rare: *T. lutescens* with an initial phase that is mainly yellow, and *T. quinquevittatum* which is complexly colored in rose and green. Hawaiian records of *T. lunare* (Linnaeus) and *T. melanochir* (Bleeker) [= *T. amblycephalum* (Bleeker)] appear to be in error.

113. *Halichoeres ornatissimus* (Garrett), 1863.   ornate wrasse, 'ōhua
Dorsal rays IX,12; anal rays III,12; pectoral rays 13; lateral-line scales 27; depth of body 3 to 3.4 in standard length; head scaleless; scales on chest much smaller than those on most of body; one canine tooth on each side of front of jaws and one at corner of mouth (posteriorly on upper jaw); pelvic fins of large males may reach origin of anal fin; caudal fin rounded. Body rose to brownish red with a green spot on each scale, often shading to whitish ventrally without markings; head with irregular bands of rose and green, the uppermost green band continuing along back where it may break into a series of spots; a small black spot behind eye; a small blackish spot at front of dorsal fin; individuals less than about 4.5 inches have a black spot as large as eye at front of soft portion of dorsal fin and those less than about 3.5 inches have a black spot on penultimate dorsal fin membrane. Reaches 6 inches. Islands of Oceania. A common inshore species in Hawaii. In its food habits it shows a preference for small benthic mollusks and crustaceans.

114. *Macropharyngodon geoffroy* (Quoy and Gaimard), 1824.   shortnose wrasse
Dorsal rays IX,11; anal rays III,11; pectoral rays 12; lateral-line scales 26 or 27; body moderately deep, 2.35 to 2.65 in standard length; snout short, 3 to 3.85 in head; head scaleless; two pairs of enlarged canines anteriorly in both jaws; a large canine at corner of mouth (posteriorly on upper jaw); caudal fin rounded. Orange-yellow with dark-edged blue spots; a black spot on lower half of first two interspinous membranes of dorsal fin. Males develop bright red and yellow pigment on the outer half of the first three dorsal fin membranes and black at the pectoral base. Largest specimen, 6.2 inches. Occurs only in the Hawaiian Islands where it is known from the depth range of 20 to at least 100 feet. Feeds primarily on mollusks and foraminifera. The generic name is derived from the large molariform teeth in the pharyngeal region which are used to crush the shells of its prey.

115. *Pseudojuloides cerasinus* (Snyder), 1904.   smalltail wrasse
Dorsal rays IX,11; anal rays III,12; pectoral rays 13; lateral-line scales 27; body slender, the depth 3.7 to 4.4 in standard length; snout moderately pointed; head scaleless; scales on chest much smaller than those of rest of body; preopercular margin smooth; a single protruding slightly outcurved canine tooth on each side at front of jaws; remaining teeth along side of jaws uniserial, almost incisiform; no tooth at corner of mouth; caudal fin short, 4.5 to 5.6 in standard length (1.5 to 1.9 in head), truncate to slightly rounded. Females light red, shading to white on lower half of body, the median fins pale yellowish. Males olive green dorsally, light blue ventrally, with a mid-lateral double stripe of bright blue and yellow; a large blue-edged black area on outer half of caudal fin; a blackish spot at front of dorsal fin. Largest Bishop Museum specimen, 4.8 inches. Indo-Pacific. Rare in less than 60 feet. Usually found on rubble bottoms; swims close to the substratum.

116. *Gomphosus varius* Lacepède, 1801.   bird wrasse, 'aki-lolo, hīnālea'i'iwi
Dorsal rays VIII,13; anal rays III (first spine slender),11; pectoral rays 16 (rarely 15 or 17); lateral-line scales 26 or 27; depth of body 3.5 to 4 in standard length; snout of adults extremely long and slender, 1.7 to 2 in head (snout not produced in small juveniles); head naked except for a few small scales on upper gill cover; preopercular margin as in *Thalassoma*; caudal fin rounded in juveniles, slightly rounded in females, and truncate to emarginate in males. The body of females is white anteriorly with a black spot on the edge of each scale, soon shading to blackish, this color continuing onto median fins except a

broad whitish border on caudal fin and a row of light yellow spots near base of anal fin; snout red dorsally shading to light reddish on upper head; head below eye and chest white; a black spot at upper pectoral base. Males are deep blue-green with a vertical red line on each body scale, a greenish yellow bar on body above pectoral base, and a large crescent of light blue green posteriorly in caudal fin; a black spot at upper pectoral base. Juveniles are green to olive on back, white below with two black stripes. Largest specimen recorded, 12.5 inches. Occurs throughout Oceania and the western Pacific. Replaced in the Indian Ocean by *G. caeruleus* Lacepède. A common inshore species in Hawaii. Stomach contents of 14 adults indicate a preferred diet of small benthic crustaceans (78% by volume, mainly crabs, shrimps, mantis shrimps, and hermit crabs), brittle stars (10%), fishes (9.5%), and mollusks. *G. tricolor* Quoy and Gaimard and *Thalassoma stuckiae* Whitley are synonyms, named for the male and juvenile forms, respectively. The Hawaiian name 'aki-lolo is applied to the female and hinalea 'i'iwi to the male.

117. *Stethojulis balteata* (Quoy and Gaimard), 1824.   **belted wrasse, 'ōmaka** Dorsal rays IX,11; anal rays III (first spine very small),11; pectoral rays 14 (rarely 15); lateral-line scales 25; gill rakers 26 to 29; depth of body 2.7 to 3.1 in standard length; head scaleless; small incisiform teeth in jaws, none notably enlarged anteriorly; a canine tooth at corner of mouth; caudal fin rounded, about 3.2 to 4.5 in standard length. Initial color phase greenish on back, finely speckled with whitish, shading to whitish ventrally; one to three (usually two) small pale-edged black spots mid-laterally on posterior caudal peduncle; a large bright yellow spot above pectoral base; base of pectoral fins blackish. Terminal males green on back, pale blue below, the two regions separated by a broad stripe of orange edged in bright blue running from axil of pectoral fin to lower caudal fin base; head with narrow bright blue bands, the uppermost running from eye across nape and continuing along back just beneath dorsal fin; caudal fin yellow; dorsal fin orange; pectoral fins with orange bar at base. Largest specimen, 5.8 inches. Restricted to the Hawaiian Islands. An abundant, active, inshore fish. Feeds mainly on pelecypods, polychaete worms, peanut worms, gastropods, various small crustaceans, and foraminifera. The prey animals are very small, generally, those with hard parts usually not crushed. Spawns both in aggregations of initial-phase individuals and in dichromatic pairs. The eggs are pelagic, about 0.5 mm in diameter. *S. axillaris* (Quoy and Gaimard) is a synonym. The related *S. albovittata* (Bonnaterre) is confined to the Indian Ocean, and *S. bandanensis* (Bleeker) to the tropical Pacific, except Hawaii.

PARROTFISHES (SCARIDAE)

The parrotfishes are well named for their bright colors and beak-like dentition formed by the fusion of teeth. Like the wrasses from which they have been derived, the juveniles are often colored differently from adults, and there are usually two strikingly different color patterns associated with sex. Many species undergo sex reversal. Typically, a female of relatively drab hue, often gray to reddish brown, changes to a male and takes on a gaudy pattern that is usually dominated by green or blue-green. These terminal males appear to have sexual territories and spawn with only a single female at any one time. In addition, for some species, there is group spawning by aggregations of like-colored fish. All of the species have an unnotched dorsal fin of IX,10 rays and an anal fin of III,9 rays. The scales are cycloid and large, usually 22 to 25 in the lateral line. The dental plates have a median suture; adults may have one or two canine teeth posteriorly on the side of the dental plates. The upper pharyngeal bone is paired, the lower single, both with rows of pavement-like molariform teeth. Parrotfishes are herbivorous, though a few species such as *Scarus perspicillatus* feed in part on live coral. With their strong dental plates these fishes are able to graze on benthic algae even when it is present only as a low stubble (thus making them superior competitors to other plant-feeding fishes). When the bottom is relatively soft rock such as dead coral, they tend to remove some of the substratum as well, leaving characteristic grooves. They grind their algal food, along with the soft rock or sediment they have ingested, in their pharyngeal mill, thus rendering it more digestible. Because of their endless scraping and the action of their pharyngeal mill they produce an enormous amount of sediment. They are more important in the production of sand in tropic seas than any other group of animals. At night they sleep on the bottom. Some species secrete around themselves a veil-like cocoon of mucus (which may be only a normal accumulation of mucus that would be swept away by day as the fish swims). Seven species of parrotfishes occur in the Hawaiian Islands. All are relatively shallow-water fishes. *Calotomus cyclurus* Jenkins, described from a single specimen from Hawaii, is a probable locality error and synonym for the Japanese *C. japonicus*. The general Hawaiian name for parrotfishes is uhu.

118. *Calotomus carolinus* **(Cuvier and Valenciennes), 1839.**

stareye parrotfish, pōnuhunuhu

Teeth readily apparent on outer surface of dental plates, imbricated, the tips of upper row giving a jagged cutting edge to the plates; edges of dental plates not clearly overlapping; depth of body 2.2 to 2.6 in standard length; pectoral rays 13; dorsal spines flexible; caudal fin slightly rounded in juveniles, truncate in subadults, and truncate with lobes slightly to moderately produced in adults. Initial color phase mottled dark orangish brown, shading to orangish ventrally; basal portion of pectoral fin dark; posterior margin of caudal fin narrowly pale. Terminal male color phase primarily blue-green with orange-pink bands radiating from eye. To 20 inches. Indo-Pacific and tropical eastern Pacific. Some authors have erroneously used the names *C. spinidens* (Quoy and Gaimard) and *C. sandwicensis* (Cuvier and Valenciennes) for this species. *C. spinidens* is a small, grass-bed parrotfish of the western Pacific and Indian Oceans; *C. sandwicensis* is a junior synonym of *carolinus*.

119. *Calotomus zonarchus* **(Jenkins), 1903.** **yellowbar parrotfish**

Dentition as in *C. carolinus*; depth of body 2.5 to 2.9 in standard length; pectoral rays 13, dorsal spines stiff, the tips sharp; caudal fin slightly rounded to truncate. Mottled orangish brown, shading to light orangish ventrally (scales light gray-green or pale bluish at edges, orangish brown in centers, with small finger-like extensions or spots of pale color running into the brown); a few scattered pale pink scales on body; a blackish spot at front of dorsal fin; anus black. Terminal males have a light orange-yellow bar on body at region of pectoral fin tip and broad irregular bars of rose on ventral half of head. Hawaiian Islands. Not common. Largest collected by author, 11.5 inches, but probably reaches about 13 inches. Formerly classified in the genus *Scaridea*, here regarded as a synonym of *Calotomus*.

120. *Scarus sordidus* **Forsskål, 1775.** **bullethead parrotfish, uhu**

No individual teeth apparent at front of dental plates; lower dental plate fitting inside upper when jaws closed; much of dental plates not covered by lips; dorsal and ventral profiles of front of head equally convex; depth of body 2.5 to 3.1 in standard length; pectoral rays usually 15; two rows of scales on cheek; caudal fin usually truncate (slightly rounded in juveniles and slightly emarginate in some large males). Juveniles and females are dark brown, the chin and lips reddish; dental plates white. Individuals in this phase can display a broad white band at caudal base containing a large brown spot; also they may exhibit a double row of widely spaced small white spots along the side. Males are predominately green with a broad yellow region over most of side of body (better developed on some individuals than others); two or three pink to lavender stripes within green ventral part of body; dental plates green; edges of lips narrowly orange, submarginally blue-green; a broad blue-green band running from corner of mouth to below eye; two green bands above this passing posteriorly from eye. Largest Hawaiian specimen at Bishop Museum, 15.5 inches. Indo-Pacific. One of the most abundant of scarid fishes throughout its vast range.

121. *Scarus perspicillatus* **Steindachner, 1879.**

spectacled parrotfish, uhu 'ahu'ula, uhu-uliuli
Dentition typical of the genus; lips not covering dental plates; front of head convex, the forehead of large males somewhat protuberant; depth of body 2.3 to 2.7 in standard length; pectoral rays usually 15; one or two rows of scales on cheek; caudal fin truncate. Females dark brown, shading to red ventrally, the caudal peduncle and scaled basal part of caudal fin abruptly whitish; fins red. Juveniles similar but with less red color, and pale posterior zone little developed. Males with scales posterior to pectoral fins blue-green, edged with orange; anterior body and scaled portion of head orange with numerous small blue-green spots and short lines except for a solid blue-green band at base of dorsal fin passing forward onto nape; narrow irregular turquoise bands on head, one enclosing a lavender bar which crosses upper snout in front of eye. Reaches nearly 2 feet. One of 21.2 inches weighed 15.5 pounds. Hawaiian Islands only. The Hawaiian name uhu 'ahu'ula is applied to the female of this species. The synonym *Scarus ahula* Jenkins was based on this color form. Uhu-uliuli is used for the blue-green male.

122. *Scarus psittacus* **Forsskål, 1775.**   **palenose parrotfish, uhu**
Dentition as in *S. sordidus* but lips nearly covering dental plates; profile of front of head not evenly convex; depth of body 2.4 to 2.9 in standard length; two rows of scales on cheek; pectoral rays usually 14; caudal fin of adults emarginate to lunate. Initial phase reddish brown, shading to reddish ventrally; pelvic fins red; a small black spot at upper base of pectoral fins. In life the dorsal part of the snout is slightly whitish. Terminal male green with an orange-pink bar at edge of scales; dorsal part of snout lavender in life; three green bands passing posteriorly from eye, the lowermost linked to a turquoise band to corner of mouth which divides to border lips; dental plates white; a large yellow area may be present posteriorly on side of caudal peduncle; a small black spot at upper base of pectoral fins. Largest Hawaiian specimen, 11.6 inches. Indo-Pacific, from the Red Sea to French Polynesia. *Scarus forsteri* Cuvier and Valenciennes is a synonym.

123. *Scarus rubroviolaceus* **Bleeker, 1849.**   **redlip parrotfish, pālukaluka**
Dental plates as in other *Scarus*; lips not covering dental plates; dorsal profile of head rising steeply from mouth to level of eye, then curving sharply, the remaining profile to dorsal fin origin nearly straight; depth of body 2.75 to 3.1 in standard length; pectoral rays usually 15; three rows of scales on cheek (usually with two scales in third row); caudal fin of adults lunate. Females brown to reddish brown, shading ventrally to red, with small black spots and irregular lines on scales of body except ventrally; fins red except lower half of pectorals which is pale; dental plates white. Males are green, the edges of the scales salmon, with a wash of this color over side of body; upper lip narrowly salmon; above this a broad zone of turquoise; lower lip and chin with a double turquoise band (separated by salmon) which continues as a single irregular band to below eye; dental plates blue-green; gill cover yellowish; caudal fin dull orange with irregular blue-green markings and broad blue upper and lower margins. In life adults are dark on head and body just posterior to pectoral fin tips, then abruptly paler posteriorly. Largest examined by author, 28 inches (12.6 pounds). Indo-Pacific and tropical eastern Pacific. *Scarus paluca* Jenkins is a synonym.

124. *Scarus dubius* Bennett, 1828.   **regal parrotfish, lauia**
  Dentition as in *S. sordidus*; lips nearly covering dental plates; depth of body 2.4 to 2.85 in
  standard length; pectoral rays 14 or 15 (usually 14); three rows of scales on cheek; caudal
  fin slightly rounded in young to very lunate in large males. Initial color phase brownish red
  (more brown dorsally, more red ventrally) with two or three pale stripes on ventral part of
  body. Terminal males yellow-orange with a blue-green bar on posterior part of body
  scales except abdomen and chest; edges of lips blue-green, the upper band continuing to
  below eye; a blue-green stripe through upper part of eye; complex turquoise markings on
  ventral part of head. Attains about 14 inches. Found only in the Hawaiian Islands. *Scarus
  lauia* Jordan and Evermann is a synonym based on the colorful male.

LEFTEYE FLOUNDERS (BOTHIDAE)

  The Bothidae is one of seven families of flatfishes, all of which have both eyes on one side of
the head. These fishes begin life as symmetrical larvae, with one eye on each side. Before they
settle out of the plankton and take up residence on the sea bottom, one eye slowly migrates
over the top of the head from one side to the other. In the case of the Bothidae, the eyes are on
the left side; there are no spines in the fins (though primitive flatfishes of the family Psettodidae
have them); the dorsal and anal fins are long, the dorsal extending forward onto the head; the
pelvic fin on the blind side is short-based; the lateral line is usually highly arched anteriorly.
These fishes normally live on sedimentary bottoms, and they may partially bury in the sand.
The blind side is usually white, the ocular side protectively colored like the substratum. These
fishes are well known for their ability to alter their color to match the adjacent benthic
environment. There are 12 species of bothid fishes in Hawaii, most of which occur at
greater-than-diving depths. Of the two commonly found in shallow water, *Bothus mancus* is
most apt to occur in and about coral reefs.

125. *Bothus mancus* (Broussonet), 1782.   **manyray flatfish, pāki'i**
  Dorsal rays 95 to 103; anal rays 75 to 80; pectoral rays 11 or 12, lateral-line scales 85 to
  90; depth of body 1.7 to 2 in standard length; anterior interorbital space unscaled. Eyes of
  adult males widely separated, and upper pectoral rays on ocular side very prolonged. Also,
  large males develop a spine on snout above upper lip, and another above front of lower
  eye. Color variable but generally mottled light brown with pale spots and three indistinct
  blackish spots in a mid-lateral row, the largest in about middle of body. Largest collected
  by author, 19 inches (3.2 pounds). Indo-Pacific and tropical eastern Pacific. Stomachs of
  22 adults opened (only three empty). Of food material, 88% was fishes; the rest consisted
  of crabs and shrimps. The closely related *B. pantherinus* (Rüppell) has fewer fin rays
  (dorsal rays 85 to 95; anal rays 64 to 72; pectoral rays 10 or 11), and the anterior
  interorbital space is scaled. The Hawaiian endemic species *B. thompsoni* (Fowler) is
  known from 236 to 370 feet; it differs in greater body depth (1.5 to 1.7 in standard length)
  and fewer lateral-line scales (usually 76 to 88).

MOORISH IDOL FAMILY (ZANCLIDAE)

  This family of fishes consists of a single genus and species, the bizarre *Zanclus cornutus*,
the characters of which are summarized below. It is classified in the suborder Acanthuroidei
of the Perciformes, along with the family Acanthuridae (surgeonfishes). These are high-

bodied compressed fishes with long nasal bones (hence the eye is well above the mouth), and small mouths. Some authors include the Siganidae (rabbitfishes) with this suborder, no members of which occur in the Hawaiian Islands.

126. *Zanclus cornutus* **(Linnaeus), 1758.** **Moorish idol, kihikihi**
Dorsal rays VII,40 to 43; anal rays III,33 to 35; pectoral rays 18 or 19; depth of body 1.0 to 1.4 in standard length; third dorsal spine extremely long and filamentous, normally longer than standard length; snout markedly produced; mouth small, the teeth slender, slightly incurved, uniserial; adults with a bony projection in front of each eye, larger in males. White anteriorly, yellow posteriorly, with two black bars, the first nearly enclosing eye, broadening ventrally to include thorax, pelvic fins, and half of abdomen; second bar on rear half of body, edged posteriorly with white and black lines, extending onto dorsal and anal fins; a black-edged orange saddle-like marking on snout; chin black; caudal fin largely black. To 8 inches. Indo-Pacific and tropical eastern Pacific. From shallow to relatively deep water; submarine observations in Hawaii to 600 feet. Omnivorous, but feeds more on animal material, especially sponges, than algae. The late postlarval stage, which was named *Chaetodon canescens* by Linnaeus, transforms to the juvenile at a large size (to over 3 inches); it has a stout curved preorbital spine on each side of head which is shed during transformation. Difficult to maintain in an aquarium.

SURGEONFISHES (ACANTHURIDAE)

The surgeonfishes, also called tangs, are readily identified by their possession of one or more spines or tubercles on the mid-side of the caudal peduncle. The species of *Acanthurus, Ctenochaetus,* and *Zebrasoma* have a single lancet-like spine which folds into a groove; the Hawaiian species of *Naso* have two fixed spines. All of these fishes should be handled with care as the caudal spines can inflict deep gashes. Surgeonfishes are capable of cutting other fishes with these spines. Generally, they only display a slight side-swipe of the tail toward an intruding fish who almost invariably withdraws. The orange spot around the caudal spine of *Acanthurus achilles* and the bright orange and blue caudal bucklers of *Naso lituratus* and *N. unicornis,* respectively, appear to be examples of warning coloration. Other family characteristics are the deep compressed body, the deep preorbital, small mouth with nonprotractile upper jaw, and a single unnotched dorsal fin. The genus *Naso* has I,3 instead of I,5 pelvic rays; some species have a prominent rostral projection or horn in front of the eyes which has led to the common name unicornfishes, whereas others such as *N. hexacanthus* do not. The family is well represented in Hawaii by 23 species. Most are herbivorous, but some species of *Naso* and *Acanthurus thompsoni* (Fowler) feed mainly on zooplankton; the two *Ctenochaetus* are primarily detritus feeders. Surgeonfish teeth are well adapted to their mode of feeding. Those of *Acanthurus,* for example, are close-set and spatulate with denticulate margins — ideal for grazing on filamentous algae. The very long digestive tract is also a specialization for plant-feeding. The postlarval stages of acanthurids are orbicular, transparent with silvery abdomen, and scaleless with narrow vertical ridges on the body; they have venomous dorsal, anal, and pelvic spines. Venomous spines are retained by adults of at least some of the species of *Naso.* At night surgeonfishes come to rest on the bottom in a state of torpor resembling sleep.

127. *Acanthurus guttatus* **Bloch and Schneider, 1801.**
whitespotted surgeonfish, 'api
Dorsal rays IX,27 to 30; anal rays III,23 to 26; pectoral rays 15 to 17; body deep, the depth 1.5 to 1.6 in standard length; caudal fin emarginate, the caudal concavity 14 to 17

in standard length. Brown with three white bars, the body posterior to middle bar with numerous small white spots; pelvic fins yellow. Largest specimen, 11.3 inches. Indo-Pacific. Lives in surge zone, often in small schools. The author has suggested that the white spots may simulate the swirling bubbles from the action of the surf, thus providing some camouflage. Browses on filamentous algae and some calcareous algae, such as *Jania*.

128. *Acanthurus triostegus* **(Linnaeus), 1758.** **convict tang, manini**
Dorsal rays IX,22 to 26 (usually 23 or 24); anal rays III,19 to 22 (usually 21); pectoral rays 14 to 16; depth of body 1.8 to 2 in standard length; caudal spine very small, about 10 in head; caudal fin slightly emarginate. Light greenish gray with six black bars (one on head through eye, four long ones on body, and a short one on caudal peduncle). Largest specimen, from Midway Island, 10.3 inches. Indo-Pacific and tropical eastern Pacific. In Hawaii the population has differentiated slightly. Instead of a short black bar, spot, or double spot at the pectoral base, Hawaiian fish have a diagonal streak which extends below the fin base; also there are modally one more dorsal and anal rays. The Hawaiian form was named by Streets (1877) as the variety *sandvicensis* which seems best applied as a subspecies. The most abundant of Hawaiian surgeonfishes; occurs in a variety of habitats from shore to about 150 feet. The diet consists of many species of filamentous algae. Often feeds in aggregations which may collectively overwhelm territorial plant-feeding fishes. Spawning has been observed at dusk; small groups of fish dart upward about 8 feet above a large milling aggregation, releasing eggs and sperm at the peak of this movement. Spawning males have broader dark bars on the body and the median fins are nearly black except for center of the caudal fin. The spawning season in Hawaii is early December to late July; most ripe female fish were obtained from 12 days before to two days after full moon. The eggs are pelagic, 0.67 mm in average diameter. The duration of larval life is about 2.5 months. Postlarvae seek the shallows, often tidepools, to transform (requires four or five days); average size at transformation, 1.25 inches. Juveniles grow 12 mm (0.5 inches) per month. Maturity is reached at a length of about 4.8 inches at which time growth has slowed to about 2 mm per month. Growth ceases for both juveniles and adults during winter months in Hawaii.

129. *Acanthurus leucopareius* **(Jenkins), 1903. whitebar surgeonfish, māikoiko**
Dorsal rays IX,25 to 27; anal rays III,23 to 25; pectoral rays 16; depth of body 1.7 to 1.85 in standard length; caudal fin emarginate, the caudal concavity 10 to 11 in standard length. Brown with faint bluish lines or rows of small spots on body; a broad white band passing diagonally downward from front of dorsal fin behind eye to lower edge of gill cover; a dark brown band of about equal width adjacent and posterior to white band; usually a white bar at base of caudal fin; a small black spot at rear base of dorsal fin. To 10 inches. Occurs as solitary individuals or in schools. Although usually found in the surge zone, there are submarine observations in Hawaii to 85 meters (278 feet). Collected only from the Hawaiian Islands, Marcus Island, Guam, southern Japan, Easter Island, Pitcairn, Rapa, the Austral Islands and New Caledonia; seemingly absent from more tropical areas. Browses on filamentous algae.

130. *Acanthurus olivaceus* **Bloch and Schneider, 1801.**
orangeband surgeonfish, na'ena'e
Dorsal rays IX,23 to 25; anal rays III,22 to 24; pectoral rays 16 or 17 (usually 17); depth of body 2 to 2.4 in standard length; caudal fin of adults lunate, the caudal concavity 4 to 5 in standard length. Grayish brown with a horizontal orange band, broadly edged in deep blue, passing posteriorly from upper end of gill opening; an orange line at base of dorsal fin; a large crescentic white area posteriorly in caudal fin. A color phase often seen has the

head and anterior half of body abruptly paler than posterior half of body. Reaches at least 12 inches. Central and western Pacific. Usual depth range about 30 to at least 150 feet. Often seen over sand bottoms near reefs, sometimes in small schools. Has a gizzard-like stomach; generally ingests some inorganic sediment with its food of diatoms, fine filamentous algae, and detritus.

131. *Acanthurus dussumieri* Cuvier and Valenciennes, 1835.

eye-stripe surgeonfish, palani

Dorsal rays IX,25 to 27; anal rays III,24 to 26; pectoral rays 16 or 17 (usually 17); gill rakers 23 to 26; depth of body 1.9 to 2.1 in standard length; large individuals with a strongly convex forehead (perhaps more characteristic of males); caudal spine large, 3 to 5 in head; caudal fin lunate in adults, the caudal concavity 7 to 9 in standard length; a gizzard-like stomach. Yellowish brown with irregular narrow blue lines on body; head yellowish with blue spots and lines, a broad yellow band across interorbital space, and a blotch of yellow behind and adjacent to eye; opercular membrane blackish; caudal spine white, the socket broadly rimmed with black; dorsal and anal fins yellow with a blue band at base, a blue margin, traces of narrow blue stripes distally (fins of young fully striped), and blue on last few rays; caudal fin blue with small blackish spots, yellow at base. Reaches at least 18 inches. Indo-Pacific, however this species appears to be absent from the central Pacific except for the Hawaiian Islands and the Line Islands. Generally seen in more than 30 feet of water; submarine observations in Hawaii to 420 feet. Usually grazes on diatoms, fine green and bluegreen algae, and detritus from sand bottoms, along with considerable sand, but occasionally browses on algae from hard substrata.

132. *Acanthurus blochii* Cuvier & Valenciennes, 1835. ringtail surgeonfish, pualu

Dorsal rays IX,25 to 27; anal rays III,24 or 25; pectoral rays 17; gill rakers 20 to 25; depth of body 1.9 to 2.1 in standard length; length of caudal spine 3 to 4.4 in head length; caudal fin lunate, the caudal concavity 6 to 10 in standard length; a gizzard-like stomach. Dark bluish or greenish gray with small faint yellowish to light gray spots forming irregular longitudinal lines on body; an elongate yellow spot extending posteriorly from lower part of eye; a margin of dark brown to black around caudal spine as broad as width of spine; usually a white band across caudal fin base; rest of fin blue with about six indistinct wavy vertical yellowish brown lines; dorsal fin with eight or nine longitudinal blue bands alternating with dull orange-yellow bands, and anal fin with five or six similar bands; pectoral fins dark bluish, without a zone of yellow. Underwater this species appears almost black except for the usual white ring around the base of the caudal fin. Attains about 17 inches. Indo-Pacific. More characteristic of clear outer-reef areas than the following species. Though closely tied to coral reefs, this fish feeds mainly over sandy areas on diatoms, detritus, etc., ingesting the usual component of sand which probably aids in the trituration of the algal food in the thick-walled stomach. Misnamed *mata* by most authors.

133. *Acanthurus xanthopterus* Cuvier and Valenciennes, 1835.

yellowfin surgeonfish, pualu

Dorsal rays IX,25 to 27; anal rays III,23 to 25; pectoral rays 16 or 17 (usually 17); gill rakers 16 to 24; depth of body 1.95 to 2.25 in standard length; caudal spine relatively small, its length 4.4 to 5.7 in head; caudal fin lunate; the caudal concavity 4.6 to 7 in standard length; gizzard-like stomach. Purplish gray, with or without very irregular longitudinal banding; caudal fin bluish gray, often with a whitish bar at base (though less distinct generally than that of *A. blochii*); often some yellow in front and behind eye but not as a distinct band as in *A. dussumieri;* dorsal and anal fins brownish yellow with three or four longitudinal blue bands; outer third of pectoral fins yellow. Largest species of the genus; attains 22 inches. Wide-ranging, from East Africa to Mexico. Occurs in harbors, bays, and deep outer reef areas (submarine observations to 300 feet), often ranging far from the shelter of reefs. Although this species has the same Hawaiian name as the closely related A. blochii, fishermen distinguish the two, calling A. xanthopterus th deep-water pualu. Food habits similar to A. blochii; occasionally caught on hook and line with animal material as bait.

134. Acanthurus achilles Shaw, 1803. achilles tang, pāku'iku'i
Dorsal rays IX,29 to 33; anal rays III,26 to 29; pectoral rays 16; depth of body 1.75 to 1.9 in standard length; caudal fin lunate, the caudal concavity 5.5 to 8 in standard length. Black with a large elliptical vivid orange spot posteriorly on body enclosing caudal spine; an elongate white spot at edge of gill cover; caudal fin with a broad middle zone of orange separated by black from the white borders. Juveniles lack the large orange spot. Largest specimen, 10 inches. Seems to be confined in its distribution to the islands of Oceania. Occurs in moderately turbulent water of exposed reefs. Browses on filamentous and small fleshy algae. An aggressive species, often driving away other surgeonfishes that venture into its territory. The late postlarval stage which has small brown spots dorsally and posteriorly on the body, is unusually large for the genus, attaining about 2.8 inches in total length. Sixth in total catch for the Hawaiian aquarium fish trade.

135. Acanthurus nigricans (Linnaeus), 1758. whitecheek surgeonfish
Dorsal rays IX,28 to 31; anal rays III,26 to 28; pectoral rays 16; depth of body 1.7 to 1.85 in standard length; caudal fin emarginate, the caudal concavity 10 to 14.5 in standard length. Black; a horizontally elongate white area below and adjacent to eye; a narrow white band nearly encircling mouth; opercular membrane yellowish; sheath and very narrow edge of socket of caudal spine yellow; caudal fin white with a yellow band in about posterior third of fin paralleling posterior border and angling anteriorly to be submarginal for a short distance in lobes of fin; a band of yellow basally in dorsal and anal fins which broadens to nearly full height of fins posteriorly. Largest specimen, 8.4. inches. Occurs throughout the tropical Pacific, including islands of the eastern Pacific; common at most archipelagos but rare in the Hawaiian Islands (most often seen at the island of Hawaii). Like the related A. achilles, it is an aggressive species of the surge zone, but generally in slightly deeper less turbulent water; submarine observations to 150 feet. Hybridizes with A. achilles. A. glaucopareius Cuvier and A. aliala are synonyms.

136. Acanthurus nigrofuscus (Forsskål), 1775. brown surgeonfish, mā'i'i'i
Dorsal rays IX,24 to 27; anal rays III,22 to 24; pectoral rays 16 or 17; depth of body 2 to 2.3 in standard length; caudal fin lunate, the caudal concavity 4.5 to 6 in standard length. Brown, suffused with lavender; head and chest with orange dots; a prominent black spot at rear base of dorsal and anal fins, the dorsal spot large, contained less than 2 times in eye diameter; lips blackish; a black edge on socket for caudal spine; posterior margin of caudal fin white (width about 2 in pupil), with a blackish submarginal line. Largest specimen, 8 inches. A common species distributed from the Red Sea and east African coast to French Polynesia; second in abundance only to A. triostegus among Hawaiian surgeonfishes. Although it may penetrate the lower part of the surge zone, it is generally found in water deeper than 15 or 20 feet. Tied closely to hard substratum for shelter and its food of filamentous algae. Sometimes misidentified as A. elongatus (Lacepède).

137. Acanthurus nigroris Cuvier and Valenciennes, 1835.
bluelined surgeonfish, maiko
Dorsal rays IX,24 to 27; anal rays III,23 to 25; pectoral rays 15 or 16; depth of body 1.8 to 2 in standard length; caudal fin emarginate, the caudal concavity 5.8 to 7.5 in standard length. Dark brown with irregular longitudinal blue lines on body; a black spot at rear base of dorsal and anal fins, the dorsal fin spot contained more than 2 times in eye diameter;

caudal fin with a narrow white posterior margin (width rarely less than 4 in pupil). Maximum length, 10 inches. Appears restricted to the islands of Oceania. Average dorsal and anal fin-ray counts of this species in Hawaii (given above) are one ray higher than other islands of the Pacific. Although generally observed on reefs or rocky substrata where it browses on filamentous algae, it will also graze on diatoms and other fine algae growing on compacted sand bottoms.

138. *Ctenochaetus strigosus* **(Bennett), 1828.** **goldring surgeonfish, kole**
Dorsal rays VIII,25 to 28; anal rays III,21 to 25; pectoral rays 16 (rarely 15); gill rakers 29 to 34; depth of body 1.7 to 2 in standard length; teeth numerous (up to 60 in upper jaw), elongate with incurved tips (denticulate on one side) and flexible in jaws; margins of lips smooth; caudal fin moderately emarginate, the caudal concavity 6 to 10 in standard length. Brown with numerous light blue longitudinal lines which extend diagonally onto basal soft portions of dorsal and anal fins; a distinctive yellow ring around eye (better developed in the population in the Hawaiian Islands than elsewhere), and faint blue dots on head; pectoral fin membranes clear. Largest specimen, 7.2 inches. Indo-Pacific; generally rare except in the Hawaiian Islands where it is abundant [which may be related to the absence of *C. striatus* (Quoy and Gaimard) in Hawaii, a species far more common than *strigosus* where the two co-exist]. Occurs from shallow reefs to at least 150 feet. Feeds on detritus by whisking its comb-like teeth over the bottom as it closes its mouth (at the same time creating suction).

139. *Ctenochaetus hawaiiensis* **Randall, 1955.** **black surgeonfish**
Dorsal rays VIII,27 to 29; anal rays III,25 or 26; pectoral rays 16; gill rakers 21 to 25; depth of body 1.75 to 2.05 in standard length; teeth as in *C. strigosus,* but not as numerous (for fish of about the same size — the number of teeth increases with age) and the uppers with fewer denticulations; margins of lips finely crenulate; caudal fin slightly emarginate, the caudal concavity 10 to 24 in standard length. Dark olive brown with fine lengthwise yellowish gray lines on the head and body. (underwater this fish appears almost black). Juveniles very different from adults, orange with bluish chevron-like markings on the side, the dorsal and anal fins elevated posteriorly, and the teeth lacking denticulations. Largest Bishop Museum specimen, 11.1 inches. When described, *C. hawaiiensis* was known only from the island of Hawaii. The author has since collected it in the Society Islands, Tuamotu Archipelago, Marquesas Islands, Pitcairn Group, Austral Islands, Samoa Islands, Marshall Islands, and Marcus Island. Deepest collection, 200 feet.

140. *Zebrasoma flavescens* **(Bennett), 1828.** **yellow tang, lau'i-pala**
Dorsal rays V,23 to 26; anal rays III,19 to 22; pectoral rays 14 to 16; depth of body 1.4 to 1.75 in standard length; dorsal fin elevated, the longest ray 2.8 to 3.8 in standard length; a dense patch of setae posteriorly on side of body; caudal fin truncate. Entirely bright yellow except for white sheath on caudal spine. Approaches 8 inches. Known from the Hawaiian Islands, Marshall Islands, Mariana Islands, Wake Island, Marcus Island, and southern Japan. From the shore (where calm) to at least 150 feet; more common on the lee side of islands. Browses on filamentous algae from hard substrata. The top marine fish in Hawaii of the aquarium fish trade (18% of total catch). The closely related *Z. scopas* (Cuvier), a dark brown species, does not occur in the Hawaiian Islands.

141. *Zebrasoma veliferum* **(Bloch), 1797.** **sailfin tang, māne'one'o**
Dorsal rays IV,29 to 33; anal rays III,23 to 26; pectoral rays 15 to 17; depth of body 1.8 to 2 in standard length; dorsal fin very elevated, the longest ray 2.1 to 2.5 in standard length; caudal fin truncate. Alternately banded with near-vertical broad bars of grayish brown and narrow ones of white, the brown bars containing brownish orange lines (broken on first two bars) and the white bars with yellow lines; snout yellowish with small pale spots; caudal

spine edged in blackish, surrounded by a broad zone of pale blue; dorsal and anal fins banded with bluish and brownish orange; caudal fin yellowish with a narrow pale blue margin. Juveniles with alternating narrow bars of yellow and black. Largest recorded specimen, 15.5 inches. Indo-Pacific. Slightly different in the Indian Ocean where some authors prefer to apply the name *Z. desjardinii* (Bennett). Found on reefs in calm bays and off exposed rocky shores, sometimes entering surge zone. Less common than *Z. flavescens;* food habits similar.

142. *Naso lituratus* (Bloch and Schneider), 1801.

orangespine unicornfish, umaumalei

Dorsal rays VI,28 to 30; anal rays II,29 to 30; pectoral rays 16 or 17; depth of body 1.9 to 2.4 in standard length; no rostral prominence on forehead; caudal spines large, forward-curved, immobile (as on all *Naso*); caudal fin lunate, large males with a long filament extending from each lobe. Grayish brown, with a curved yellow band from corner of mouth to eye; snout in front of band black; lips orange; a large area of yellow behind and above eye; caudal spines and a broad area around each bright orange; dorsal fin black basally (broader anteriorly), white outwardly, with a narrow black margin and a blue line at extreme base; anal and pelvic fins yellow. Reported to 18 inches. Indo-Pacific. Feeds mainly on leafy brown algae such as *Sargassum, Pocockiella,* and *Dictyota.* Juveniles of this *Naso* comprise the fourth largest catch of the aquarium fish trade in Hawaii.

143. *Naso unicornis* (Forsskål), 1775.   **bluespine unicornfish, kala**

Dorsal rays VI,27 to 30; anal rays III,27 to 30; pectoral rays 17 or 18; depth of body 1.8 to 2.6 in standard length; adults with a prominent horn projecting anteriorly from between eyes, but not extending before mouth; profile from mouth to base of horn forming an angle of about 45°; caudal spines large, forward curved; caudal fin emarginate in young, developing long slender lobes in adults. Light olive to yellowish gray, the caudal spines and a small area around each bright blue; dorsal and anal fins with alternating narrow bands of light blue and brownish yellow, diagonal in dorsal fin and longitudinal and wavy in anal fin, both fins with bright blue margins. Reported to 27 inches. Indo-Pacific. Feeds predominately on coarse leafy algae, particularly the same three genera of browns as listed above for *N. lituratus.* Often seen foraging for food in small groups, sometimes in surprisingly shallow water for such large fishes.

144. *Naso hexacanthus* (Bleeker), 1855.   **sleek unicornfish, kala holo**

Dorsal rays VI,27 to 29; anal rays II,28 to 30; pectoral rays 17 or 18 (usually 17); depth of body 2.6 to 3 in standard length; no rostral prominence on forehead; caudal spines only slight keels until large size attained; caudal fin emarginate to nearly truncate. Brownish gray, shading ventrally to yellowish, but in life the color can vary from dark brown to pale blue; opercular membrane dark brown; dorsal and anal fins yellowish with indistinct diagonal brown bands and narrow blue margins. Attains about 30 inches. Indo-Pacific in distribution. Not common in less than about 50 feet, but abundant in its habitat in deeper water; submarine observations in Hawaii to 450 feet. Generally seen in aggregations near escarpments; feeds on zooplankton, especially the larger animals such as crab larvae, arrow worms, and pelagic tunicates.

145. *Naso brevirostris* (Cuvier and Valenciennes), 1835.

spotted unicornfish, kala lōlō

Dorsal rays VI,27 to 29; anal rays II,27 to 30; pectoral rays 15 or 16 (usually 16); depth of body 2.4 to 2.7 in standard length; a bony horn on head projecting anteriorly at level of eye (only a bump on the young, very long on adults — well in front of mouth); profile from mouth to base of horn nearly vertical; caudal spines slow to develop, as in the preceding species; caudal fin slightly rounded. Brownish gray, sometimes with a bluish cast, darker dorsally than ventrally, with numerous small dark brown spots (more evident on pale ventral part of body). Reported to reach 2 feet. Broadly distributed in the Indo-Pacific from the Red Sea and East Africa to French Polynesia and the Pitcairn Group. Occurs from depths of about 20 to at least 150 feet. Juveniles and subadults browse on benthic algae, but adults feed on zooplankton; perhaps the development of the rostral prominence in front of the mouth dictates the change in food habits. The scientific name *brevirostris* was based on a subadult with a short horn. Another unicornfish with a horn, *Naso annulatus* (Quoy and Gaimard), is rare in Hawaii; it is distinctive in having V dorsal spines and a broad white posterior border on the caudal fin.

GOBIES (GOBIIDAE)

The Gobiidae is a very large family of small fishes. Typically they are carnivorous and bottom-dwelling. Those for which reproduction has been studied lay demersal adhesive eggs which are guarded by the male parent. The majority have the pelvic fins united to form a sucking disc. There are two dorsal fins, the first fin of II to VIII slender spines, the second and the anal fin preceded by a weak spine. Twenty-seven species of gobies occur in the Hawaiian Islands in a variety of habitats including fresh water *(Sicyopterus, Awaous, Lentipes)*, the intertidal zone *(Bathygobius, Kelloggella)*, on or near coral reefs *(Eviota, Priolepis, Gnatholepis, Fusigobius, etc.)*, and deep water *(Oxyurichthys* sp.). Some live in close association with other animals; examples are *Bryaninops yongei* (Davis and Cohen) with an antipatharian sea whip and *Psilogobius mainlandi* Baldwin with a snapping shrimp. Because of their small size, gobiid fishes tend to be overlooked by most snorkelers or divers. The general Hawaiian name for gobies and the related sleepers (Eleotrididae) is 'o'opu.

146. *Asterropteryx semipunctatus* **Rüppell, 1830.** **bluespotted goby, 'o'opu**
Dorsal rays VI-I,9 to 11; anal rays I,8 to 10; pectoral rays 17; pelvic fins not united; scales ctenoid, 25 or 26 between gill opening and caudal fin base; head scaled except interorbital space, snout, and chin; depth of body 3 to 3.5 in standard length; preopercle with three to five short spines at angle; mouth oblique, the lower jaw protruding; conical teeth in bands in jaws, the outer row at the front enlarged (especially those in lower jaw); first three dorsal spines elongate, the third the longest; caudal fin rounded, shorter than head. Gray, usually with a broad diffuse dark stripe on upper side; head, body, and median fins with bright blue dots. Reaches about 2 inches in length. Indo-Pacific. Common on silty sand bottoms in and about shallow reefs in bays and lagoons. Often mistakenly classified in the Eleotrididae because of the divided pelvic fins; however, this is not a valid family characteristic as some gobies within a genus may have divided and others united pelvic fins.

147. *Priolepis eugenius* **Jordan and Evermann, 1903.** **noble goby, 'o'opu**
Dorsal rays VI-I,11; anal rays I,9; pectoral rays 20; pelvic fins united to form a sucking disk, the fourth rays the longest; scales ctenoid, 28 or 29 between upper end of gill opening and caudal fin base; head without scales except postorbital region, including upper half of gill cover; depth of body 3.35 to 3.8 in standard length; mouth oblique, the lower jaw protruding; dentition similar to the preceding species; fringe-like lines of papillae on head, mostly on lower half; caudal fin rounded, shorter than head. Light brown with broad brown bars on body and narrower bars on head; median fins dark brown; pelvic fins dark brown, paler at edges. Largest specimen, 2.2 inches. A common species in Hawaii where it appears to be endemic. Usually classified in *Quisquilius*.

148. *Ptereleotris heteroptera* (Bleeker), 1855.   **indigo hover goby**
Dorsal rays VI-I,27 to 32; anal rays I,24 to 30; pectoral rays 21 to 26; pelvic fins not united; scales cycloid, nonoverlapping, partially embedded, and very small, over 100 in series between gill opening and caudal fin base; head without scales except nape; body elongate, the depth 6.2 to 7.1 in standard length; mouth oblique, the lower jaw protruding; teeth in irregular rows in jaws, those in the outer row enlarged as canines (also some in inner row of lower jaw); caudal fin emarginate, longer than head. Blue, shading to whitish on lower head and abdomen; caudal yellowish with a horizontally elongate blackish spot in middle of fin. Largest Bishop Museum specimen, 4.7 inches. Known until recent years only from Borneo; the author has collected it in the Line Islands, Society Islands, Marquesas, Samoa, Marshalls, Marianas, Solomons, Maldives, Seychelles, Réunion, and the Hawaiian Islands where it is occasionally seen on rubble and sand bottoms in about 60 to 120 feet. With the approach of danger it retreats to hover over a burrow into which it will dart head first if frightened further. Often one sees two adults occupying the same burrow. Feeds on zooplankton, generally 2 to 10 feet above the bottom.

BLENNIES (BLENNIIDAE)

The blennies are small, agile, benthic fishes. All are scaleless, and most are blunt-headed. Many, such as species of *Istiblennius* and *Entomacrodus,* live on rocky shores; some are adapted to the rigorous life of the surf-swept intertidal zone. The common name rockskipper is often applied to those with the ability to leap from one pool to another. A subfamily, the saber-tooth blennies, are represented by three species in Hawaii, two in the genus *Plagiotremus* (*Runula* is a synonym), and one in *Omobranchus.* These little fishes are named for the pair of enormous curved canine teeth in the lower jaw which are used for defense. The pelvic fins of blennies are distinctly anterior to the pectorals, and the number of rays is reduced from the usual I,5 of percoid fishes to I,2 to I,4 (the pelvic spine is very small; dissection is often necessary to see it and to make an accurate ray count). There is a single dorsal fin with from III to XVII flexible spines which may be deeply notched between the spinous and soft portions; often the last dorsal ray is joined by a membrane to the upper part of the caudal peduncle (and for many species to the caudal fin as well); soft rays of fins simple except some species with branched caudal rays. All have II anal spines (though one may be embedded in females); in mature males these are usually capped by fleshy tissue which is believed to secrete an attractant when the fish are reproductively active. The mouth is low on the head; the teeth are numerous, slender, close-set, and either fixed or movable in the jaws. Blennies lay demersal adhesive eggs which are guarded by the male parent (at least for those species of which the reproductive habits have been studied). Fourteen species of Blenniidae are known from the Hawaiian Islands, of which the seven most frequently seen in the intertidal and reef habitats are discussed below.

149. *Entomacrodus marmoratus* (Bennett), 1828.   **marbled blenny, pāo'o**
Dorsal rays XIII,14 to 16 (rarely 14); anal rays II,15 to 17 (rarely 15); pectoral rays 14, the lower rays thickened; pelvic rays I,4; depth of body 4.0 to 4.9 in standard length; no crest on head; teeth movable in jaws except for a small canine posteriorly in lower jaw; small teeth present on vomer; an elongate flat tentacle over each eye with branches along the edges; two cirri on nape, the more medial one usually with branches (lateral cirrus sometimes lacking in juveniles); edge of upper lip entirely crenulate. Ground color variable but most often olive brown, mottled with white, shading to white on abdomen; a series of irregular dark brown bars on about lower two-thirds of body which tend to follow

the muscle segments; a dark shoulder spot (green on some individuals); a series of blackish spots along base of dorsal fin; blackish spots and markings on head sometimes forming bars, the most evident a near-vertical black streak just behind eye. Largest specimen from Midway, nearly 6 inches. Found only in the Hawaiian Islands. Occurs along rocky shores exposed to surf; escapes the full force of the waves by dwelling in holes and cracks in the rocks. If frightened it may leap into the swirling white water and skitter over the surface to another rock or cross in a series of leaps interspersed with short swims. Feeds primarily on detritus and algae. One other species of *Entomacrodus* occurs in Hawaii, *E. strasburgi* Springer. It is a smaller fish, reaching only about 2 inches in length, has but a single cirrus on each side of the nape, and lacks a dark mark behind the eye.

150. *Istiblennius zebra* (Vaillant and Sauvage), 1875.   **zebra blenny, pāo‘o**
Dorsal rays XIII (rarely XII or XIV),21 to 23, the last ray joined to upper caudal fin by a membrane; anal rays II,21 to 23; pectoral rays 14; pelvic rays I,3; body elongate, the maximum depth 4.5 to 5.7 in standard length; teeth movable in jaws; no canines; no teeth on vomer; a median fleshy crest on head (larger in males); a long simple tentacle over eye; no cirri on nape; edge of upper lip smooth. Color varying from nearly black through gray to light tan with dark double-bars on side of body and a series of dark blotches along base of dorsal fin and adjacent back; dorsal fin of large males often blotched with red. Largest specimen, 7.6 inches, from Laysan. Known only from the Hawaiian Islands; a close relative. *I. edentulus* (Bloch and Schneider), ranges throughout the rest of the Indo-Pacific *I. zebra* lives along exposed rocky shores from the highest tidepools to the surf zone. A very agile fish with remarkable leaping ability, it can move with rapidity in a series of jumps from pool to pool, at times over considerable stretches of dry terrain. In the highest pools it is subject to great fluctuations in temperature, salinity, oxygen content, and pH. Eggs are laid in crevices, the nests with from 1,200 to 10,000 eggs, guarded by the male parent. Nests may be found throughout the year, but peak reproduction occurs in spring and early summer. Hatching takes place in about two weeks. The advanced larval stage returns to shore for transformation from a pelagic existence of unknown duration at a standard length of about 20 mm (0.8 inches). Juveniles and subadults grow at an average rate of 5.3 mm (0.21 inches) per month. Maturity is attained at a standard length of 70 to 90 mm (2.75 to 3.5 inches). Feeds on detritus and benthic algae. One other species of the genus occurs in Hawaii, *I. gibbifrons* (Quoy and Gaimard), which is readily distinguished by its prominent overhanging forehead, lack of a crest on the head, and a short canine tooth in the lower jaw.

151. *Exallias brevis* (Kner), 1868.   *shortbodied blenny,* **pāo‘o kauila**
Dorsal rays XII,12 or 13 (usually 13); anal rays II,13 or 14; pectoral rays 15, the lower rays thickened; body relatively deep, 2.6 to 2.7 in standard length; cirri in a transverse band across nape; a branched supraorbital tentacle present; a pair of small barbels on chin; teeth in lower jaw more-or-less rigid; teeth in upper jaw movable; no canine or vomerine teeth. Ground color whitish, the head, body, and all fins covered with dark spots which tend to clump on body (except chest and abdomen) into groups of three to 12; spots on females dark brown; spots on males posterior to about mid-base of spinous portion of dorsal fin and origin of anal fin orange-red; spots and rays on dorsal and caudal fins of males red; modified anal spines of male deep indigo blue. Reaches 6 inches. Indo-Pacific; occurs in from 2 to 80 feet, but generally seen in 10 to 25 feet. Not abundant but conspicuous because of its color pattern and rather large size for a blenny. An obligate coral-polyp feeder; does not do well in an aquarium. The eggs, which are laid in small crevices, are bright yellow.

152. *Cirripectes vanderbilti* (Fowler), 1938.   **scarface blenny**
Dorsal rays XII,14 (rarely 13 or 15), the fin deeply notched between spinous and soft portion; anal rays II,15 (rarely 14 or 16); pectoral rays 15, body robust, the depth 3.2 to 3.5 in standard length; a transverse row of 31 to 44 small cirri on nape; tentacle over eye with multiple branches from base; no barbels on chin; teeth flexible in jaws; a fixed canine tooth posteriorly and medially on each side of lower jaw; no vomerine teeth; upper half of caudal fin truncate, lower half rounded. Usually dark brown, often with orange-red markings on head; dorsal and anal fins dusky except outer anterior part of dorsal which is abruptly clear. Largest specimen in Bishop Museum, 3.8 inches. Hawaiian Islands. The most common blenny on shallow reefs; usually found within the depth range of 2 to 30 feet. Feeds on benthic algae and detritus. Closely related to *C. variolosus* (Cuvier and Valenciennes) from elsewhere in the Indo-Pacific.

153. *Cirripectes obscurus* (Borodin), 1927.   **gargantuan blenny**
Dorsal rays XII,15 or 16 (rarely 15), the fin deeply notched; anal rays II,15 to 17 (rarely 15, usually 17); pectoral rays 15 (rarely 14 or 16), the lower rays thickened; body robust, the depth 3.1 to 3.3 in standard length; cirri in a transverse row on nape totaling 38 to 48; tentacle over eye with numerous branches from base; no barbels on chin; margins of lips strongly crenulate; teeth in jaws slightly movable; a fixed canine tooth posteriorly and medially on each side of lower jaw; no teeth on vomer; caudal fin slightly rounded, with greater convexity in lower half. Orangish brown, usually with numerous pale yellowish dots on head, body (generally more anteriorly), and bases of dorsal and anal fins; rays of dorsal and caudal fins reddish (especially spinous portion of dorsal); outer anterior part of dorsal fin not abruptly clear; a black spot behind eye; a male pattern of rose head and anterior body shading to rosy brown with eight broken olive bars on the side has been reported. Exceeds 7 inches in length, thus perhaps the largest of the genus. Native to the Hawaiian Islands. A species of the surge zone, hence from near shore to about 20 feet. A third species of *Cirripectes*, *C. quagga* (Fowler and Ball), occurs in Hawaiian waters. It is characterized by having modally 15 dorsal soft rays and 16 anal rays, a total of 25 to 32 nuchal cirri (distinctly interrupted in median line), usually a simple supra-orbital tentacle (if multifid, all branches from axis of tentacle and never more than five), no dark spot behind eye, the anterior outer part of the dorsal fin and upper caudal fin with pale membranes, and three to five irregular rows of well-spaced pale dots on body.

154. *Plagiotremus ewaensis* (Brock), 1948.   **Ewa blenny**
Dorsal rays X to XII (usually XI),34 to 36, the fin unnotched; anal rays II,31 to 33; pectoral rays 12 or 13 (usually 12); body very slender, the depth 6.2 to 7.9 in standard length; no cirri or tentacles on head; mouth ventral, the conical snout overhanging; teeth in jaws incisiform except for an enormous curved canine tooth posteriorly on inside of lower jaw which fits into a socket at side of roof of mouth; caudal fin emarginate. Orange-yellow with two narrow bright blue stripes edged in blackish, which narrow as they pass onto head, one just above eye and the other through lower part of eye; a median blue line on head; dorsal and anal fins orange to red-orange, the tips of the rays bright blue with a submarginal blackish line; caudal fin clear yellow with dusky rays. Reaches a length of 4 inches. Endemic to the Hawaiian Islands where it is known from the depth range of 30 to 180 feet. Very close to *P. rhynorhynchos* (Bleeker) which is found throughout the rest of the Indo-Pacific; some might prefer to regard *ewaensis* as a subspecies of *rhynorhynchos*. The species of *Plagiotremus* feed by making rapid attacks on other fishes from which they remove epidermal tissue, small scales, and mucus. They generally hover one to a few feet above the reef waiting for unwary prey to come near enough for them to reach with a burst of speed. They often attack divers, the result being little more than a light touch (which

nevertheless can be unnerving when unexpected). The large canines are not used for feeding but for protection and territorial defense. These blennies will seek shelter in empty worm or gastropod tubes which they enter tail-first. They are poor subjects for aquaria as it is difficult to induce them to accept ordinary fish food; instead, they persist in feeding on the skin of the other piscine inmates.

155. *Plagiotremus goslinei* (Strasburg), 1956. **scale-eating blenny**
Dorsal rays VIII (rarely VII),34 to 37; anal rays II,28 to 31 (modally 29); pectoral rays 12; body very slender, the depth 6.6 to 8.3 in standard length; no cirri or tentacles on head; mouth ventral, the conical snout overhanging; teeth in jaws incisiform except for an enormous curved canine posteriorly on inside of lower jaw which fits into a socket at side of roof of mouth; dorsal fin unnotched; caudal fin emarginate. Greenish on back, white ventrally, the two zones separated by a stripe which is orange-yellow on head and blackish on body (where it may consist of a series of indistinct conjoined spots). A small species; attains only 2.5 inches. Hawaiian Islands. Not uncommon from the shallows to about 50 feet. Very closely related to *P. tapeinosoma* (Bleeker) from elsewhere in the Indo-Pacific; a strong case could be made to classify *goslinei* as a subspecies of *tapeinosoma*. See discussion under *P. ewaensis* for habits.

FILEFISHES (MONACANTHIDAE)

The filefishes (called leatherjackets in Australia) are named for their tough shagreen-like skin. The scales are not overlapping; each has a group of small spinules except at the edges, which tend to obscure the scale outlines. These fishes have two dorsal fins, the first consisting of a long spine on the head (usually bearing small spines or tubercles) that can be locked into an erect position by a rudimentary second spine. The body is deep and compressed. The snout is often produced and the mouth small; the jaws, however, are powerful and the teeth chisel-like and sharp, six in each jaw, the uppers reinforced by an inner row of four. There are no pelvic fins; instead there is a single small spinous knob called the pelvic terminus (rudimentary or absent on *Aluterus*) at the end of the long pelvic bone. The depth of the body can be increased by the depression of this bone and stretching of the loose skin on the pelvic flap. The uppermost pectoral ray is very short; it is nonetheless included in the pectoral counts below. The gill opening is reduced to a small slit on the side. There are eight species of this family in Hawaii. Not included herein are the deepwater *Thamnaconus garretti* (Fowler) and the two large circumtropical species of *Aluterus*: the blue-spotted *A. scriptus* (Gmelin) which has a very long rounded caudal fin; and the drab *A. monoceros* (Osbeck) with a short slightly emarginate caudal fin. Both are rare in Hawaii. None of the filefishes are strong swimmers; their usual mode of progression consists of undulating the second dorsal and anal fins. The monacanthid fishes are sometimes combined with the closely related triggerfishes into a single family. Together with the trunkfishes, puffers, porcupinefishes and molas they are grouped in the order Tetraodontiformes (Plectognathi); these are among the most highly evolved of fishes.

156. *Cantherhines sandwichiensis* (Quoy and Gaimard), 1824.
squaretail filefish, 'ō'ili-lepa
Dorsal rays II-33 to 36; anal rays 30 to 32; pectoral rays 13 to 15; depth at origin of anal fin about 2.4 in standard length; first dorsal spine over eye, with tiny blunt spinules or tubercles, fitting into a deep groove in back when depressed; pelvic terminus fixed; setae

posteriorly on body poorly developed; caudal fin truncate (slightly rounded if broadly spread). Brown to gray, sometimes with indistinct small pale spots; a white spot (prominent in life) below rear base of second dorsal fin and a smaller less distinct but comparable spot above rear base of anal fin; lips blackish; broad region of head around eye with alternating narrow bands of yellowish and pale bluish; first dorsal and caudal fins dark brown, the caudal rays yellowish distally; remaining fins with nearly clear membranes and orange-yellow rays. Largest collected by author, 7.6 inches. Hawaiian Islands. Feeds principally on algae and detritus, but also ingests tunicates, corals, sponges, and other benthic animals. Closely related to *C. pardalis* (Rüppell) from elsewhere in the Indo-Pacific region. Another Hawaiian endemic species, *C. verecundus* E. K. Jordan differs in its rounded caudal fin and shorter first dorsal spine (about 1.4 in snout; the spine of *C. sandwichiensis* and *C. dumerilii* is about equal to the snout length).

157. *Cantherhines dumerilii* (Hollard), 1854. barred filefish, 'ō'ili

Dorsal rays II-34 to 39; anal rays 28 to 35; pectoral rays 16 (rarely 15); depth at origin of anal fin about 2.3 in standard length; first dorsal spine similar to that of *C. sandwichiensis;* pelvic terminus fixed; two pairs of prominent forward-curving spines laterally on caudal peduncle (larger on males); caudal fin rounded. Grayish brown with about 12 indistinct narrow dark brown bars on posterior two-thirds of body; caudal spine bases bright orange; lips flesh-colored to whitish, edged with blackish; dorsal, anal, and pelvic fins with yellow rays; caudal fin orange, the rays sometimes dusky basally. Juveniles and subadults may have small white spots. Largest collected, 14.8 inches. Feeds mainly on branching corals, but echinoids, bryozoans, and other benthic animals are occasionally eaten. East Africa to tropical America; not uncommon. *C. carolae* Jordan and McGregor and *C. albopunctatus* (Seale) are synonyms.

158. *Pervagor spilosoma* (Lay and Bennett), 1839. fantail filefish, 'ō'ili-'uwī'uwī

Dorsal rays II-37 to 39 (usually 38); anal rays 34 to 36 (usually 35); pectoral rays 14 to 16; depth at origin of anal fin about 2.4 to 2.7 in standard length; first dorsal spine over eye, bearing a row of prominent downcurved spines on each side, not folding into a deep groove in back; pelvic terminus movable; setae on scales longer on posterior part of body; caudal fin rounded. Body yellowish with numerous small black spots; head yellow, shading anteriorly to gray, with narrow diagonal black bands; caudal fin orange, finely spotted with black basally, with a broad black submarginal band and a narrow yellow margin. Largest Bishop Museum specimen, 7.1 inches. Size at transformation from late postlarval stage to the juvenile 2.1 to 2.4 inches. Hawaiian Islands. Generally common from shallow water to 150 feet, but varies in abundance over the years. Stomach contents of seven adults consisted of algae and detritus (68.5%), pelecypods, gastropods, ostracods, tunicates, sponges, heart urchins, foraminifera, and shrimps; also reported to feed on corals.

159. *Pervagor aspricaudus* (Hollard), 1854. lacefin filefish

Dorsal rays II-31 to 34; anal rays 28 to 31; pectoral rays 12 to 14; depth of body at origin of anal fin 2.4 to 2.7 in standard length; first dorsal spine over eye, bearing a row of prominent downcurved spines on each side, and not folding into a deep groove in back; pelvic terminus movable; long setae on scales posteriorly on body, producing a brush-like effect; caudal fin rounded. Light grayish brown with a fleck of black on each scale, thus forming fine irregular dotted lines on body, shading posteriorly to orange; an area of blackish on head above eye which passes from behind and adjacent to eye to upper end of gill opening; lips blackish; a submarginal blue line on pelvic flap; caudal fin bright orange with a narrow blue margin and two irregular broken blue submarginal lines; first dorsal fin dark brown with a few scattered blue dots; second dorsal and anal fins light orangish with longitudinal rows of blue dots; pectoral fins pale with blue dots at base. Largest Hawaiian specimen, 4.5 inches; largest from all localities, 7.1 inches. Indo-Pacific. Far less common than *P. spilosoma*. Bishop Museum specimens from Hawaii have been collected in the depth range of 6 to 50 feet. Previously identified as *P. melanocephalus* (Bleeker), now known to be a different species restricted to the western Pacific.

TRIGGERFISHES (BALISTIDAE)

These fishes share many features with the filefishes. They have a similar body shape, lack pelvic fins, have a long depressible pelvic bone, and a first dorsal spine which can be locked in position by the small second spine (the "trigger," for if it is moved downward the first spine can be depressed). The first spine is stouter than that of filefishes, and there is a small third dorsal spine. When danger threatens, a triggerfish may retreat to a hole in the reef with a small entrance, erect its first dorsal spine and lower the pelvic bone, thus wedging itself in position. Observations suggest that one hole in the reef is the preferred refuge, and it is this place to which a triggerfish retires at night (balistids are active by day, quiescent at night). The triggerfishes have a tough skin like the filefishes with scales which do not overlap, but the projections in the central part of each are short and the outlines of the scales more apparent. The dentition is almost the same; there are eight outer teeth in each jaw, the uppers buttressed by an inner row of six teeth. The small but powerful jaws and sharp teeth enable these fishes to feed on a variety of invertebrates with hard parts. They are, therefore, not compatible with certain invertebrates in aquaria; also, they can be damaging to other fishes in a tank. Like the filefishes they swim by undulation of the second dorsal and anal fins, bringing the caudal fin into action only when they wish to move rapidly. Ten balistid fishes are known from the Hawaiian Islands. Omitted are the pelagic *Canthidermis maculatus* (Bloch), the rare *Xanthichthys mento* (Jordan and Gilbert), and the very rare *Pseudobalistes polylepis* Steindachner, a large plain-colored species which is common in the eastern Pacific. Those few individuals of *P. polylepis* taken in Hawaii are probably not representative of a local population but strays from the eastern Pacific. All of the balistid species in Hawaii except those of the genus *Xanthichthys* have curious bony plates behind the gill opening and all but *Rhinecanthus* have a deep groove in front of the eye. Counts of pectoral rays include the very short rudimentary upper ray.

160. *Rhinecanthus rectangulus* (Bloch and Schneider), 1801.
reef triggerfish, humuhumu-nukunuku-a-puaʻa

Dorsal rays III-23 to 25; anal rays 21 or 22 (usually 21); pectoral rays 13; dorsal and ventral profiles of head nearly straight; depth at anal fin origin 2.6 to 3 in standard length; caudal peduncle with three or four rows of small forward-curved spines; caudal fin slightly rounded to double emarginate; second dorsal and anal fins not elevated anteriorly. Brown, shading to white on lower head and abdomen, with a black band from eye which broadens and angles diagonally backward, enclosing pectoral fin base, and ending at anus and anterior three-fourths of anal fin base; (this band is bordered anteriorly on near vertical part to pectoral base by two blue bands and on upper edge of posterior diagonal part by gold); a large gold-bordered triangular black spot with base on caudal peduncle and apex on side between middle of second dorsal and anal fins; a gold band above and parallel to upper leg of black triangle, linking to gold border of diagonal black band; a broad blue band containing three black lines across interorbital space; a transverse blue band above upper lip; a red bar at base of pectoral fin. Reaches 10 inches. Indo-Pacific. Common in the shallow outer reef habitat; not easily approached underwater. Stomach contents of 12 specimens revealed feeding on a great variety of small benthic organisms: algae and detritus (18.5%), crabs (13.5%), polychaete worms (9.5%), brittle stars (9%), sea urchins and heart urchins (6.5%), gastropods (5.5%), peanut worms (5%), pelecypods (4%), tunicates, mantis shrimps, shrimps, isopods, amphipods, copepods, foraminifera, eggs, ostracods, and sponges. Recently selected as the state fish of Hawaii.

161. Rhinecanthus aculeatus (Linnaeus), 1758.

lagoon triggerfish, humuhumu-nukunuku-a-pua'a
Dorsal rays III-24 to 26; anal rays 21 to 23; pectoral rays 13 or 14; dorsal and ventral profiles of head nearly straight; depth of body at origin of anal fin 2.5 to 3 in standard length; caudal peduncle with three rows of small forward-curving spines; caudal fin slightly rounded to double emarginate; dorsal and anal fins not elevated anteriorly. Light brown dorsally, shading to white ventrally, with a large blackish area containing four pale bluish diagonal bands from mid-side to anal fin; an orange-yellow area around mouth and anterior snout containing a transverse blue band above upper lip and continuing as a diagonal band to below pectoral base; four blue lines across interorbital space and three curved blue lines from eye to pectoral base, the posterior two enclosing a blackish bar; caudal spines black, surrounded by pale bluish; a blackish area around anus. Reported to 12 inches. Indo-Pacific. Prefers a lagoon or protected bay environment. Not common in Hawaii. Omnivorous; stomach content analyses revealed feeding on algae, detritus, mollusks (both gastropods and pelecypods), crabs, shrimps, and other crustaceans, polychaetes and other worms, heart urchins, fishes, corals, tunicates, foraminifera, and unidentified eggs.

162. Xanthichthys auromarginatus (Bennett), 1831.   gilded triggerfish
Dorsal rays III (third dorsal spine very small)-27 to 30; anal rays 25 to 27; pectoral rays 13 to 15; rows of scales on head from corner of mouth to upper end of gill opening 17 to 20; dorsal and ventral profile of head convex; five longitudinal grooves separating scale rows on cheek, passing from below corner of mouth nearly to upper pectoral base (grooves better developed on the other four species of the genus, some with only three); depth of body at origin of anal fin 2.45 to 2.7 in standard length; median longitudinal ridges along scale rows posteriorly on body well developed; caudal fin deeply emarginate; second dorsal and anal fins elevated anteriorly. Brownish gray with a bluish or lavender cast, the scales of the lower half or more of body with a whitish spot; margins of second dorsal, anal and caudal fins dark reddish brown on females and bright yellow on males; males with a blue patch on the head below level of mouth. Largest Hawaiian specimen, 7.7 inches. Recorded also from Mauritius, Réunion, Maldive Islands, Nicobar Islands, Cocos-Keeling Islands, Ryukyu Islands, and Marshall Islands. Specimens have been collected from depths of 40 to 150 feet (mostly from 100 feet or more), but the species undoubtedly ranges into deeper water. Feeds on zooplankton, especially calanoid copepods. One other member of the genus occurs in Hawaii, X. mento (Jordan and Gilbert), but it is rare; it has 29 to 32 rays in the second dorsal fin, 26 to 29 rays in the anal fin, 19 to 22 head scale rows, and a more elongate body (depth 2.85 to 3.45 in standard length).

163. Sufflamen bursa (Bloch and Schneider), 1801. lei triggerfish, humuhumu lei
Dorsal rays III-27 to 29; anal rays 24 to 26, pectoral rays 13 or 14; depth at origin of anal fin 2.4 to 2.8 in standard length; dorsal and ventral profiles of snout nearly straight; each longitudinal row of scales on body with a median series of tubercles which coalesce posteriorly on body to form ridges bearing forward-curving spines; caudal fin truncate to slightly rounded; second dorsal and anal fins slightly elevated anteriorly. Grayish brown, often abruptly whitish below a white line from corner of mouth to anal fin origin; pelvic terminus and edge of ventral flap to anus black with a white submarginal line; a scimitar-

shaped dark brown bar from in front of lower pectoral fin base through posterior part of eye; a second pointed dark bar passing upward and diagonally backward from pectoral base. Reaches 8.5 inches. Indo-Pacific. Moderately common in Hawaii from 10 to at least 300 feet. Stomach contents of 14 adult specimens consisted of algae and detritus (17%), crabs (15%), pelecypods (12.5%), gastropods (9.5%), heart urchins and sea urchins (7.5%), polychaetes (6%), peanut worms (5.5%), damselfish and other eggs, tunicates, chitons, amphipods, isopods, shrimps, and unidentified small crustaceans. Sometimes called the scythe triggerfish.

164. *Sufflamen fraenatus* **(Latreille), 1804. bridled triggerfish, humuhumu-mimi**
Dorsal rays III-28 to 30; anal rays 25 to 27, pectoral rays 14 to 16 (usually 15); depth of body at origin of anal fin 2.1 to 2.7 in standard length; dorsal and ventral profiles of head nearly straight; a tubercle or spinule on each scale on posterior half of body; caudal fin rounded in juveniles, truncate to slightly double emarginate in adults; second dorsal and anal fins slightly elevated anteriorly. Brown with a pale yellowish to whitish line on head running posteriorly and slightly downward from corner of mouth toward lower pectoral base, this line linked to one on the other side by a similar line under the chin; lips and a narrow zone around mouth bluish except for a band of yellow basally on lower lip. Juveniles are dark brown on about upper fifth of head and body, pale brown below, with lengthwise dark brown lines along side of body (some interrupted) and irregular lines ventrally and on head; a black spot on first interspinous membrane of dorsal fin. Reported to reach 15 inches. Indo-Pacific. Bishop Museum specimens have been collected in the depth range of 25 to 350 feet. The stomach contents of ten adult specimens consisted of sea urchins and heart urchins (20.4% by volume) including *Diadema, Eucidaris,* and *Echinometra;* fishes (18.9%) including *Gymnothorax;* pelecypods (13.9%); tunicates (10%); brittle stars (7.4%); crabs (7.1%); mantis shrimps (3.5%); algae and detritus (3.1%); polychaete worms, shrimps, gastropods, sponges, amphipods, bryozoans, foraminifera, and ostracods. *Sufflamen capistratus* (Shaw) is a synonym.

165. *Melichthys vidua* **(Solander), 1844. pinktail durgon, humuhumu-hi'u-kole**
Dorsal rays III-31 to 35; anal rays 28 to 31, pectoral rays 14 to 16; rows of scales on head between corner of mouth and upper end of gill opening 28 to 32; dorsal and ventral profiles of head convex; depth of body at origin of anal fin 2.3 to 2.6 in standard length; scales posteriorly on body with a slight mid-longitudinal ridge; caudal fin truncate to slightly emarginate; second dorsal and anal fins distinctly elevated anteriorly. Dark brown, often with a yellowish cast; scaled basal part of caudal fin white, remaining part pink, the upper and lower edges of fin narrowly black; second dorsal and anal fins whitish with black borders; pectoral fins yellow. Largest specimen, 13.4 inches. Indo-Pacific. Not uncommon on Hawaiian reefs; submarine observations to 460 feet. Feeds mainly on algae and detritus but also consumes crabs and other crustaceans, octopuses, sponges, and fishes. The species of *Melichthys* transform from the late postlarval form to the juvenile at a large size; that of *vidua* to 6.2 inches. *Balistes nycteris* (Jordan and Evermann) was based on a transforming specimen; this form lacks the black border to the second dorsal and anal fins, but has several narrow black longitudinal bands within the fins.

166. *Melichthys niger* **(Bloch), 1786. black durgon, humuhumu-'ele'ele**
Dorsal rays III-30 to 34; anal rays 28 to 30; pectoral rays 15 to 17; rows of scales on head between corner of mouth and upper end of gill opening 20 to 25; dorsal and ventral profiles of head convex; depth of body at origin of anal fin 2.4 to 2.8 in standard length; prominent longitudinal ridges following scale rows posteriorly on body; caudal fin of adults deeply emarginate to lunate; second dorsal and anal fins distinctly elevated anteriorly. Dark blue-green in life with black longitudinal lines and a narrow light blue

band at the base of the second dorsal and anal fins. Upon death the ground color becomes almost uniformly black. Largest specimen examined, 12.5 inches, from Laysan, Hawaiian Islands. Circumtropical, varying greatly in abundance from area to area. Algae is the principal food (about 70% of the volume of the stomach content material), some of it being taken as drifting fragments and some grazed from the bottom; the remaining food is mainly zooplankton. This fish generally maintains a position in the water column well above the bottom. It is very wary and quickly retreats to its hole in the reef with the approach of danger. *Melichthys radula* (Solander) and *M. piceus* (Poey) are synonyms.

TRUNKFISHES (OSTRACIIDAE)

The trunkfishes, sometimes called boxfishes, are unique in the possession of an armor-like carapace of bony polygonal plates with gaps for the mouth, gill opening, anus, caudal peduncle, and fins. The surface of the carapace may be rough due to the presence of small tubercles. There is a single dorsal fin posterior in position and no pelvic fins. There are six species in Hawaii: the six-angled *Aracana aculeata* (Houttuyn) from deep water, two cowfishes *(Lactoria)* with a forward-projecting spine in front of each eye, and three *Ostracion*. The most common Hawaiian trunkfish is *O. meleagris*, discussed below.

167. *Ostracion meleagris* **Shaw and Nodder, 1796.**   **spotted trunkfish, moa**
Dorsal rays 9; anal rays 9; pectoral rays 10; carapace quadrangular in cross-section, the sides slightly concave and the dorsal and ventral surfaces convex except posteriorly on ventral surface where it is concave; no spines on carapace. Juveniles and females dark brown with small white spots, more numerous in larger adults. Males colored like females dorsally on body but with fewer and larger spots; sides blue or blue-gray with small blackish spots (about six to eight per hexagonal plate) except for a row of dark-edged orange-yellow spots along the upper ridge of the carapace and upper caudal peduncle; a large pale pinkish area usually present under eye. Largest specimen, 6.2 inches. Indo-Pacific and tropical eastern Pacific. The Hawaiian population has differentiated in color from the species elsewhere in the Indo-Pacific. Away from Hawaii juveniles and females have more white spots at any one size, and the males have large dark-edged orange-yellow spots on the sides. The name *camurum* Jenkins, 1901 may be used as a subspecies for the form in Hawaii. *O. lentiginosus* Bloch and Schneider and *O. sebae* Bleeker are synonyms of *meleagris*, the former named for the male phase. Feeds primarily on sponges, algae, and tunicates (mainly didemnids). This fish, and probably other trunkfishes as well, secretes a toxic substance (named ostracitoxin) under stress which may be lethal to other fishes maintained in confinement in the same water. *O. whitleyi* Fowler, a rare species in Hawaii, is also sexually dichromatic, the females brown with white spots and a broad white stripe on lower side; the males are white-spotted on the back but deep blue on the side with a black-edged white stripe on upper side and a dark-edged white bar running ventrally from posterior part of eye. A third species, *O. cubicus* Linnaeus, is known from only a single subadult specimen from Hawaii collected in the 1920's, and doubt of the validity of this record has been expressed; however, a recent sight record of a juvenile, unmistakable in its bright yellow black-spotted color pattern, establishes the species as occurring in Hawaii, though probably only as a stray.

168. *Lactoria fornasini* **(Bianconi), 1846.**   **thornback cowfish, makukana**
Dorsal rays 9; anal rays 9; pectoral rays 11 (rarely 12); carapace basically quadrangular in cross-section but a median ridge and large thorn-like spine in the middle of the back

nearly qualify it as five-sided; the lateral sides are concave and strongly flaring outward ventrally to form a pronounced acute ventro-lateral ridge which ends posteriorly in a stout backward-projecting spine; bottom of carapace convex; a stout sharp spine extending anteriorly from supraorbital ridge (an anterior extension of the dorso-lateral ridge of body); the five carapace spines of juveniles are relatively longer than those of adults, and the spines in front of the eyes angle upward and outward; gill opening a short vertical slit just in front of upper base of pectoral fin; caudal fin rounded. Light brown to tan with large diffuse dusky blotches and scattered light blue spots and short lines; joints of polygonal plates of carapace (which vary from quadrangular to hexagonal) blackish; fins pale. Reported to 6 inches; largest Bishop Museum specimen, 5.5 inches, from Seychelles (most Hawaiian specimens much smaller). Occurs in the Indian Ocean, the western Pacific from Queensland, East Indies, and Japan, and the Hawaiian Islands. Apparently unknown from other localities in Oceania. Observed more on rubble and sand bottoms than coral reefs. Occurs from about 20 to at least 100 feet. The Bishop Museum has three night-light collections of specimens taken by dip net in early June which range from 0.7 to 1.1 inches; also there is one collection of the same size range taken from the stomach of a mahimahi (*Coryphaena hippurus* Linnaeus) in February. The second species of *Lactoria* in Hawaiian waters, *L. diaphanus* (Bloch and Schneider), is rare; it is distinctive in having one or more spines on the dorso-lateral ridge posterior to the head; also it reaches larger size — up to 12 inches.

PUFFERS (TETRAODONTIDAE)

The puffers or blowfishes are named for their capacity to inflate themselves by drawing water into the abdomen. They are characterized by having a tough skin (often with small spinules), beak-like dental plates in each jaw (plates with a median suture), small gill opening, a single posterior dorsal fin, and no pelvic fins. The puffers are well known for the toxicity of their tissues. The viscera, including the gonads, and the skin are the most toxic parts. The musculature is safer and is generally considered a delicacy, but even it may be poisonous. These fishes are most dangerous to eat immediately prior to and during the spawning season. The toxicity varies greatly with the species and with area. Relatively few cases of puffer poisoning have been reported from the Hawaiian Islands, but deaths have occurred. Twelve species of puffers are known from Hawaii, seven of which are in the genus *Canthigaster*. The small colorful fishes of this genus, popularly called tobies or sharpnose puffers, are sometimes classified in a separate family, but recent authors regard them as a subfamily of the Tetraodontidae.

169. *Canthigaster amboinensis* (Bleeker), 1865.   Ambon toby
Dorsal rays 11 or 12 (usually 12); anal rays 10 or 11 (usually 11); pectoral rays 16 or 17; depth of body 2.3 to 2.5 in standard length. Olivaceous with small light blue to white spots on body (and base of caudal fin) except ventrally and small dark spots about the same size but more elongate (most apparent on lower half of body, especially upper abdomen where they extend slightly lower than blue spots); blue lines radiating from eye; cheek light yellowish with small blue spots or lines. Largest, 5.2 inches. Indo-Pacific and tropical eastern Pacific. Ranges into shallower water, often subject to surge, than other species of the genus. Feeds principally on algae (43.5% of contents of 12 stomachs), but also eats polychaete worms, sea urchins, brittle stars, mollusks, tunicates, corals, crustaceans, and sponges.

170. *Canthigaster jactator* (Jenkins), 1901.   Hawaiian whitespotted toby
Dorsal rays 8 to 10; anal rays 8 to 10; pectoral rays 16 to 18; depth of body 2.3 to 2.7 in
standard length. Brown with white spots (relatively smaller and more numerous on larger
fish); fins pale, without spots. Largest specimen, 3.5 inches. Known only from the
Hawaiian Islands, where it is the most common member of the genus, at least in shallow
water. Very closely related to *C. janthinopterus* (Bleeker) from elsewhere in the Indo-
Pacific region and to *C. punctatissimus* (Günther) the eastern Pacific. It differs from both
notably in having fewer and larger white spots. Analysis of the stomach contents of
18 adults revealed feeding on sponges (37.5%), algae and detritus (22%), tunicates
(13.5%), polychaete worms, bryozoans, sea urchins, brittle stars, crabs, peanut worms,
shrimps, zoanthids, fishes, amphipods, and foraminifera.

171. *Canthigaster coronata* (Vaillant and Sauvage), 1875.   crown toby
Dorsal rays 9 or 10; anal rays 9 or 10; pectoral rays 16 or 17; depth of body 2.6 to 2.9 in
standard length. White with scattered yellow dots, a black bar across interorbital, and three
black bars on upper half of body which are broader dorsally (the first vertical, the second
oblique, and the last very oblique, the lower end of this bar anterior to dorsal and anal fins
and the upper end on caudal peduncle and base of caudal fin); yellow and blue lines
radiating from eye. Largest specimen, 5.3 inches. Most commonly seen below depths of
75 feet (deepest collected from a dredge haul in 258-396 feet), but occasionally sighted in
as little as 20 feet. Indo-Pacific, but not known from most island groups of Oceania.
Stomach contents of 12 adults consisted of a great variety of benthic organisms: gastropods (15% by volume), sponges (14.5%), algae (12%), pelecypods (11%),
polychaetes (10%), tunicates (7.5%), crabs, sea urchins, heart urchins, brittle stars,
bryozoans, peanut worms, various small custaceans, and foraminifera. *C. cinctus* Jordan
and Evermann is a synonym.

172. *Canthigaster epilampra* (Jenkins), 1903.   lantern toby
Dorsal rays 10; anal rays 9; pectoral rays 16 to 18; depth of body 2.5 to 2.7 in standard
length. Whitish with numerous blue dots on body; a large black spot usually present at
base of dorsal fin; snout yellow with dark-edged blue spots and lines; region around eye
yellow with seven to 12 dark-edged blue lines radiating from eye; a yellow spot edged
narrowly in black and blue often present above pectoral base. Largest specimen, 4.3
inches. Described from Maui, and until recently believed confined to the Hawaiian Islands.
The author, however, has collected it in the Society Islands, Cook Islands, Marshall
Islands, Palau Islands, Solomon Islands, Philippines, and Taiwan. A relatively deep-water
species, generally seen at depths greater than 80 feet, but has been collected in as little as
20 feet.

173. *Canthigaster rivulata* (Schlegel), 1850.   maze toby
Dorsal rays 9 or 10 (usually 10); anal rays 9 or 10 (usually 10); pectoral rays 16 to 18;
depth of body 2.6 to 3.0 in standard length. Light yellowish brown on back with a reticular
network of dark blue, bluish white ventrally with faint yellow spots; two brown stripes
containing yellow dots on side of body (the upper more evident) passing from pectoral
region to caudal peduncle, the stripes joining each other in an arc in front of gill opening;
median fins yellow, striped with blue. On juveniles the two brown stripes on the side are
dark brown; on large adults they are faint. Largest specimen, 7.7 inches. Recorded from
several Indian Ocean localities, the western Pacific and the Hawaiian Islands. A species of
moderate to deep water (deepest collection 1170 feet), but the young may be common in
shallow water (in some years abundant). *C. bitaeniata* (Jenkins) is a synonym based on the
juvenile stage.

174. *Arothron hispidus* (Linnaeus), 1758.   **stripebelly puffer, keke**
Dorsal rays 10 or 11; anal rays 10 or 11; pectoral rays 17 to 19; bony rim of orbit projecting above interorbital level. Olive to gray on back with scattered white spots, shading to white on sides and ventrally, with black and pale circles around pectoral base; stripes usually present on abdomen. Largest collected by author, 19 inches. Indo-Pacific and tropical eastern Pacific. May be found in various habitats from coral reefs to estuaries. Displays an extremely varied diet: algae (including *Jania* and *Halimeda*), detritus, pelecypods, gastropods, tunicates, sponges, corals, zoanthid anemones, crabs, tube worms, sea urchins, brittle stars, starfishes (including *Acanthaster*), hermit crabs, and hydroids. The Hawaiian name makimaki has also been applied to this fish, no doubt referring to its potentiality to cause death if its viscera are eaten. However, the authenticity of this name has been questioned. In Hawaiian, death is make, not maki. If altered to makemake, the meaning is very different — desire or wish.

175. *Arothron meleagris* (Bloch and Schneider), 1801. **spotted puffer, 'o'opu-hue**
Dorsal rays 11 or 12; anal rays 12 or 13; pectoral rays 18 or 19; bony rim of orbit not raised above level of interorbital space. Brown with numerous small white spots on head, body, and median fins; outer edges of fins often pale. A color phase which is entirely bright yellow may occasionally be seen. Largest Bishop Museum specimen, 13.5 inches. Indo-Pacific and tropical eastern Pacific. Less common than *A. hispidus,* but associated more with coral reefs. Feeds mainly on corals (77% of stomach and gut contents of six adult specimens), but also ingests sponges, mollusks, bryozoans, tunicates, foraminifera, algae and detritus.

PORCUPINEFISHES (DIODONTIDAE)

These fishes are similar to the puffers, differing notably in having prominent spines that cover much of the head and body. The spines may be three-rooted, hence fixed (seen on *Chilomycterus*), or two-rooted and movable (as on *Diodon*). Normally, the spines of *Diodon* lie against the body, the tips pointing backwards, but when the fishes inflate themselves, the spines are erected to approximate right angles — an obvious deterent to a potential predator. Porcupinefishes differ further from puffers in having larger eyes, broader pectoral fins (often with the posterior edge emarginate), and lacking a median suture in their stout dental plates. Their strong beak-like jaws are admirably suited to crush the hard tests of sea urchins, shells of mollusks, and exoskeletons of crabs which are their principal sources of food. Three diodontid fishes occur in the Hawaiian Islands, two in the genus *Diodon* and one in *Chilomycterus,* the rare *C. affinis* Günther.

176. *Diodon hystrix* Linnaeus, 1758.   **porcupinefish, kōkala**
Dorsal rays 14 to 16; anal rays 14 to 16; pectoral rays 22 to 25; spines in middle of front of head not long, shorter than longest spine posterior to pectoral fins. Olive to light brown dorsally with small black spots, shading to white ventrally; fins yellowish with small black spots. Largest specimen, 28 inches. Circumtropical. Appears to be primarily nocturnal; often seen hiding beneath ledges during the day. The alimentary tracts of 12 adult specimens were examined for food. Three were empty. The remaining nine contained by volume: gastropods (42.3%), crabs (27.3%), hermit crabs (14.9%), sea urchins and sand dollars (13.7%), pelecypods (1.7%), and a few foraminifera.

177. *Diodon holocanthus* **Linnaeus, 1758.**   **spiny puffer, 'o'opu okala**
Dorsal rays 13 to 15; anal rays 13 or 14; pectoral rays 22 to 25; spines at middle of front head longer than longest spines posterior to pectoral fins. Light olive to light brown, shading to white ventrally, with a few scattered dark brown spots; a dark brown bar above and below eye; a transverse dark brown bar on occipital region of head; a large elongate dark brown spot above pectoral fins; a dark brown spot surrounding and extending onto base of dorsal fin. Attains about 15 inches. Circumtropical. More apt to enter other habitats than coral reefs than *D. hystrix*. Food habits similar to *hystrix*, feeding principally on mollusks, echinoids, crabs, and hermit crabs.

GLOSSARY

Adipose fin: a small fleshy fin without rays found on the back behind the dorsal fin of some primitive teleost fishes such as the lizardfishes.

Aglomerular: in reference to a kidney lacking glomeruli (a glomerulus is an encapsulated cluster of arterioles from which fluid containing waste material passes to kidney tubules).

Algae: a collective term for a large grouping (seven phyla) of lower plants, including seaweeds (but not seagrasses), some freshwater species, and a few semi-terrestrial forms. The singular is alga.

Alimentary tract: the digestive tract, beginning with the mouth and ending with the anus.

Amphipod: a small crustacean of the order Amphipoda characterized by lacking carapace and usually having a compressed body.

Anemone: a sessile, soft-bodied, cylindrical marine animal of the class Anthozoa, phylum Coelenterata, with a central mouth and a peripheral zone of tentacles possessing stinging cells.

Anterior: toward the front or head end of an animal.

Antipatharian: a plant-like animal of phylum Coelenterata, order Antipatharia, with a horny axial skeleton and small polyps bearing six tentacles; popularly known as black corals.

Anus: the posterior external opening of the digestive tract from which wastes are voided; sometimes called the vent.

Arrow worm: a small, slender, transparent, arrow-shaped, nonsegmented, pelagic marine animal of the phylum Chaetognatha; not a true worm.

Auxiliary scales: small scales found basally on the large scales of the head or body of a fish.

Axil: the acute angular region between a fin and the body; usually used in reference to the underside of the pectoral fin toward the base. Equivalent to the armpit of man.

Axillary: in reference to the axil.

Bar: an elongate color marking of vertical orientation, the sides of which are usually more-or-less straight (although they need not be parallel).

Barbel: a slender tentacle-like protuberance of sensory function which is found on the chin of some fishes such as goatfishes.

Benthic: closely associated with the bottom; used to categorize an aquatic organism that is attached to or resides on or near the substratum.

Bifid: divided into two equal parts or lobes; often used in reference to the distal ends of cirri or teeth of fishes.

Biogeography: the branch of biology concerned with the global distribution of plants and animals.

Biota: a collective term for the plant and animal life of a given region.

Black coral: an antipatharian (order of Coelenterata); not a true coral.

Branchiostegal rays: slender bones which support the gill membranes; sometimes referred to simply as branchiostegals.

Brittle star: one of a group of benthic marine animal of the class Ophiuroidea, phylum Echinodermata, which consist of a central disk and nearly uniform, narrow, radiating arms. Named for the fragility of the arms.

Bryozoan: a sessile plant-like animal (sometimes called moss animal) of the phylum Bryozoa; nearly all are marine and most are colonial.

Canine: a prominent, slender, sharp-pointed tooth.

Carapace: the outer bony shell of certain animals; most commonly used in reference to the shell of turtles or crabs, but also applied to the external armor-like covering of trunkfishes (Ostraciidae).

Carnivore: a flesh-eating animal.

Caudal concavity: the horizontal distance between the shortest and longest fin rays of an emarginate, lunate or forked caudal fin.

Caudal fin: the tail fin. The term tail alone generally refers to that part of a fish posterior to the anus.

Caudal peduncle: the part of the body between the posterior basal parts of the dorsal and anal fins and the base of the caudal fin. The usual vertical measurement is the least depth; the length measurement herein is horizontal, and the fin of reference (*i.e* rear base of dorsal or anal) is designated.

Cephalopod: a member of an advanced group of mollusks, the order Cephalopoda, which includes the eight-armed octopuses and ten-armed squids.

Chemosensory: in reference to a neural receptor which responds to specific chemical substances.

Chiton: a sessile marine mollusk of the class Amphineura characterized by eight external transverse calcareous plates.

Ciguatera: poisoning from the ingestion of a wide variety of tropical reef fishes; sporadic in occurrence both spatially and temporally.

Circumpeduncular: around the caudal peduncle; usually used in reference to scale counts.

Circumtropical: occurring world-wide throughout the tropic zone.

Cirrus: a small, slender, flexible, fleshy protuberance; the plural is cirri.

Compressed: laterally flattened; often used in reference to the shape of the body — in this case deeper than wide.

Conical: resembling a cone in shape; a descriptive term for teeth.

Copepod: one of a group of small crustaceans, subclass Copepoda, which are among the most abundant of pelagic marine animals; may be free-living, commensal, or parasitic.

Crustacean: in reference to arthropod animals of the class Crustacea which includes crabs, shrimps, lobsters, etc.

Ctenoid scales: scales of bony fishes which have tiny tooth-like projections along the posterior margin and part of the exposed portion. Collectively these little teeth (or ctenii) impart a rough texture to the surface of the scales.

Cuticle: the outer part of the skin of an animal which is sometimes shed.

Cycloid scales: scales of bony fishes, the exposed surfaces and edges of which lack any small tooth-like projections; they are therefore smooth to the touch.

Demersal: occurring on the bottom; often used in reference to the eggs of fishes which are attached to the substratum.

Depressed: dorso-ventrally flattened. The opposite in body shape of compressed.

Depth: a vertical measurement of the body of a fish; most often employed for the maximum height of the body excluding the fins.

Diatom: a microscopic alga of the phylum Chrysophyta characterized by silicious cell walls in two parts; unicellular or colonial; a major component of the phytoplankton.

Distal: outward from the point of attachment; the opposite of proximal.

Diurnal: in reference to an animal which is active during daylight hours.

Dorsal: of or pertaining to the back or upper part of an animal; the opposite of ventral.

Dorsal fin: a median fin along the back which is supported by rays. There may be two or more dorsal fins, in which case the most anterior one is designated the first.

Double emarginate: biconcave; used to describe the shape of the posterior edge of the caudal fin in which there are two curved indentations separated by a convexity.

Echinoid: a benthic marine animal of the class Echinoidea, phylum Echinodermata, characterized by a circular or elliptical hard outer test (shell) and numerous sharp spines; includes sea urchins, heart urchins, and sand dollars.

Ectoparasite: an organism living on another organism to its detriment. When the host is a fish, an ectoparasite (generally a crustacean, fluke, or leech) may live not only on the skin but also within the mouth or gill chamber.

Emarginate: concave; used to describe the posterior border of a caudal fin which is inwardly curved.

Endemic: restricted to a specific locality or area; indigenous.

Euphausid: a member of the marine crustacean order Euphausiacea characterized by a carapace covering all the thorax, biramous thoracic appendages and stalked eyes. The food of baleen whales known as krill are euphausids.

Exoskeleton: the outer hard structural part of certain invertebrate animal groups such as crustaceans.

Family: a major category in the classification of organisms representing a group of related genera. The suffix for animal families is "idae".

Foraminifera: an order of single-celled amoeboid animals of phylum Protozoa commonly having a many-chambered calcareous shell.

Forked: inwardly angular; used in describing the shape of a caudal fin which is divided into two equal lobes, the posterior border of each of which is relatively straight.

Fusiform: spindle-shaped; used in reference to the body shape of a fish which is cylindrical or nearly so and tapers toward the ends.

Gastropod: a marine animal of the order Gastropoda, phylum Mollusca, the benthic members of which have a muscular foot on which they adhere to and move about on the substratum; most have an external protective shell. Includes snails, abalones, limpets, cowries, nudibranchs, etc.

Genus: the name given to a group of similar species, the first part of the two-part scientific name given to all recognized animals and plants. The plural is genera.

Gill arch: the bony support for the gill filaments and gill rakers. Normally there are four pairs of gill arches in bony fishes.

Gill filaments: numerous slender vascular projections of the gill arches where the gaseous exchange of respiration takes place.

Gill membranes: membranes along the ventral and posterior margin of the operculum (gill cover) which function in respiration; they are supported by the branchiostegal rays.

Gill opening: the opening posteriorly and often also ventrally on the head of fishes where the water of respiration is expelled. Bony fishes have a single such opening on each side whereas cartilaginous fishes (sharks and rays) have five to seven. The gill openings of sharks and rays are called gill slits.

Gill rakers: stout protuberances of the gill arch on the opposite side from the red gill filaments which function in retaining food organisms. They vary greatly in number and length and are important in the classification of fishes.

Gorgonian: a plant-like animal of the order Gorgonacea, class Anthozoa, phylum Coelenterata characterized by polyps with eight tentacles and an axial skeleton of calcareous spicules; often called horny corals; includes sea fans, sea whips, etc.

Head length: the straight-line measurement of the head taken from the front of the upper lip to the membranous posterior end of the operculum.

Heart urchin: a member of the class Echinoidea, phylum Echinodermata, with an elliptical or heart-shaped shell; typically found buried in sediment.

Herbivore: a plant-feeding animal.

Hydroid: an aquatic animal of the order Hydroida, class Hydrozoa, phylum Coelenterata with tentacles around the mouth that bear stinging cells; solitary or colonial, with or without a medusa stage.

Incisiform: chisel-like; used to describe teeth which are flattened and truncate with sharp edges like the front teeth of some mammals such as man.

Indo-Pacific: the biogeographic region comprising the tropical Indian Ocean and western and central Pacific Ocean.

Initial phase: the first adult color phase of a sexually dichromatic species of fish; also known as the primary phase.

Interopercle: one of the bones comprising the operculum; bordered antero-dorsally by the preopercle and postero-dorsally by the opercle and subopercle.

Interorbital space: the region on the top of the head between the eyes; measurements may be taken of the least width, either fleshy (to the edges of the orbits) or bony (between the edges of the frontal bones which rim the orbits).

Invertebrates: animals without a backbone; hence all animals except mammals, birds, reptiles, amphibians, and fishes.

Isopod: a crustacean of the order Isopoda characterized by having a carapace, the body usually dorso-ventrally depressed, and the abdomen short with the segments partly or completely fused; marine, freshwater, or terrestrial; includes pill bugs, gribbles, etc.

Labial: referring to the lips.

Lateral: referring to the side or directed toward the side; the opposite of medial.

Lateral line: a sensory organ of fishes which consists of a canal running along the side of the body and communicating via pores through scales to the exterior; functions in perceiving low frequency vibrations, hence provide a sense which might be termed "touch at a distance."

Lateral-line scales: the pored scales of the lateral line between the upper end of the gill opening and the base of the caudal fin. The count of this series of scales is of value in the descriptions of fishes. So also at times is the number of scales above the lateral line (to the origin of the dorsal fin) and the number below the lateral line (to the origin of the anal fin).

Leptocephalus: the elongate, highly compressed, transparent larval stage of some primitive teleost fishes such as the tarpon, bonefish and eels.

Lower limb: refers either to the horizontal margin of the preopercle or to the number of gill rakers on the first gill arch below and including the one at the angle.

Lunate: sickle-shaped; used to describe a caudal fin which is deeply emarginate with narrow lobes.

Mantis shrimp: a member of the Stomatopoda, an order of marine crustaceans, the most characteristic feature of which is the enlarged first thoracic appendage, the distal segment of which closes on the next segment like the blade of a pocket knife.

Maxilla: a dermal bone of the upper jaw which lies posterior to the premaxilla. On the higher fishes the maxilla is excluded from the gape and the premaxilla bears the teeth.

Medial: toward the middle or median plane of the body; opposite of lateral.

Median: referring to the plane in the mid-line of a bilaterally symmetrical animal; the opposite of lateral.

Median fins: the fins in the median plane, hence the dorsal, anal and caudal fins.

Median predorsal scales: the number of scales running in a median row anteriorly from the origin of the dorsal fin.

Megalops: the last larval stage of a crab.

Molariform: shaped like a molar, hence low, broad and rounded.

Mollusk: a member of the phylum Mollusca, a large group of unsegmented animals usually protected by a shell of one or more parts; includes snails, clams, octopuses, chitons, etc.

Monotypic: in reference to a taxonomic group represented by a single unit of the lesser category, such as a genus of a single species or a family of a single genus.

Morphology: the branch of biology dealing with the form and structure of organisms.

Mysid: a representative of a group of small shrimps, the most distinctive feature of which is the pair of oval statocysts in the uropods (paddle-like tail appendages); popularly called opossum shrimps.

Naked: scaleless.

Nape: the dorsal region of the head posterior to the occiput.

Nasal flap: a small projection of membranous tissue at the posterior or dorso-posterior edge of the anterior nostril of fishes.

Nocturnal: in reference to an animal which is active at night.

Occiput: the region of the head above the cranium and posterior to the eye.

Ocellus: an eye-like marking with a ring of one color surrounding a spot of another.

Omnivore: an animal which feeds on both plant and animal material.

Opercle: the large bone which forms the upper posterior part of the operculum; often bears one to three backward-directed spines in the higher fishes.

Opercular membrane: the membrane at the posterior edge of the operculum of fishes, hence at the margin of the gill opening.

Operculum: gill cover; comprised of the following four bones: opercle, preopercle, interopercle and subopercle.

Ophiuroid: a member of the echinoderm class Ophiuroidea; popularly known as brittle stars.

Orbital: referring to the orbit or eye.

Order: a major category of organisms between the family and the class; a group of related families. The names of fish orders end in "iformes".

Origin: the beginning; often used for the anterior end of the dorsal or anal fin at the base. Also used in zoology to denote the more fixed attachment of a muscle.

Ostracod: a representative of the crustacean subclass Ostracoda, a group of very small aquatic animals that are protected by a two-part carapace; most live on or near the bottom.

Paired fins: collective term for the pectoral and pelvic fins.

Palatine: a paired lateral bone on the roof of the mouth lying between the vomer and the upper jaw; the presence or absence of teeth on this bone is of significance in the classification of fishes.

Papilla: a small fleshy protuberance; the plural is papillae.

Pectoral fin: the fin usually found on each side of the body behind the gill opening; in primitive fishes this pair of fins is lower on the body than in more advanced forms.

Pedicellariae: tiny pincerlike appendages of certain echinoderm animals (two-jawed in starfishes and three-jawed in sea urchins) which serve to keep the body free of debris or settling organisms or may help on the capture of prey or in defense (some are venomous). The singular is pedicellaria.

Peduncular: in reference to the caudal peduncle of fishes.

Pelagic: living in the open sea (hence some distance from land).

Pelecypod: a marine animal of the order Pelecypoda, phylum Mollusca, characterized by having two like shells (hence often called a bivalve); includes clams, mussels, oysters, etc.

Pelvic fin: one of a pair of juxtaposed fins ventrally on the body in front of the anus; varies from abdominal in position in primitive fishes such as herrings to the more anterior locations termed thoracic or jugular in advanced fishes. Sometimes called ventral fin.

Pelvic flap: the extensible ventral part of the body of filefishes and triggerfishes between the pelvic terminus and anal region.

Pelvic terminus: the small external spinous knob generally found at the end of the long pelvic girdle of triggerfishes and filefishes; it is unpaired and usually movable.

Perciform: pertaining to the Perciformes, a large order of fishes (see discussion of Serranidae).

Pharyngeal: referring to the pharynx, the region of the alimentary tract of an animal between the mouth and esophagus.

Phylum: the largest grouping in the classification of the Animal and Plant Kingdoms; the plural is phyla.

Phylogenetic: pertaining to the evolution and relationships of organisms.

Plankton: aquatic plants and animals which drift passively in open water.

Polychaete worms: a class of segmented worms (phylum Annelida), mostly marine, which possess numerous bristle-like setae extending laterally from the segments. Some polychaetes are freely mobile on the substratum, some are buried in sediment, some live in tubes of their own making, and a few are pelagic.

Polyp: the soft cylindrical body of coelenterate animals such as anemones and corals which is fixed at one end and has a mouth surrounded by tentacles at the other.

Portunid: a member of the Portunidae, a group of crabs with the fifth pair of legs modified for swimming; often the carapace is pointed at each side.

Posterior: toward the tail of an animal; opposite of anterior.

Postlarva: the stage in the development of a fish after the yolk is utilized and before it takes on an appearance similar to a juvenile.

Predorsal scales: scales anterior to the origin of the dorsal fin.

Premaxilla: the more anterior bone forming the upper jaw. In the higher fishes it extends backward and bears all of the teeth of the jaw. It is this part of the upper jaw which can be protruded by many fishes.

Preopercle: a boomerang-shaped bone, the edges of which form the posterior and lower margins of the cheek region; it is the most anterior of the bones comprising the gill cover. The upper vertical margin is sometimes called the upper limb, and lower horizontal edge the lower limb; the two limbs meet at the angle of the preopercle.

Preorbital: the first and usually the largest of the suborbital bones; located along the ventroanterior rim of the eye. Sometimes called the lacrymal bone.

Principal caudal rays: the caudal rays which reach the terminal border of the fin; in those fishes with branched caudal rays, the count includes the branched rays plus the uppermost and lowermost rays which are unbranched.

Produced: projecting or elongate.

Proximal: toward the center of the body; the opposite of distal.

Ray: the supporting bony elements of fins; includes spines and soft rays.

Rhomboid: wedge-shaped; refers to a caudal fin shape in which the middle rays are longest and upper and lower portions of the terminal border of the fin are more-or-less straight; essentially the opposite of forked. An uncommon fin shape most often found in the croakers and flatfishes.

Rostral: of or pertaining to the snout or forehead of an animal.

Rounded: refers to a caudal fin shape in which the terminal border is smoothly convex.

Rudiment: a structure so deficient in size that it does not perform its normal function; often used in reference to the small nodular gill rakers at the ends of the gill arch.

Sea urchin: a representative of the class Echinoidea of the phylum Echinodermata characterized by a circular calcareous shell and numerous radiating spines.

Serrate: notched along a free margin, like the edge of a saw.

Sessile: in reference to an organism which is attached at the base.

Seta: a bristle-like projection; the plural is setae.

Sexual dichromatism: a condition wherein the two sexes of the same species are of different color.

Simple: not branched, in reference to fin rays.

Siphonophore: a complex colonial pelagic animal of the order Siphonophora, class Hydrozoa, phylum Coelenterata; often a float at the upper end and bearing powerful stinging cells; includes the Portuguese man-of-war.

Sipunculid: a worm-like unsegmented marine animal of the phylum Sipunculida, characterized by an introvert which reveals the mouth surrounded by small lobes or tentacles when everted. Found buried in sediment or in burrows in dead coral; popularly called peanut worms.

Snout: the region of the head in front of the eye. Snout length is measured from the front of the upper lip to the anterior edge of the eye.

Soft ray: a segmented fin ray which is composed of two closely joined lateral elements. It is nearly always flexible and often branched.

Species: a population of an animal or plant which share many features (morphological, ecological, physiological, behavioral, etc.); the individuals of a species are capable of naturally interbreeding with one another. The species name is the second part of the two-part scientific name of an organism.

Spine: an unsegmented bony process consisting of a single element which is usually rigid and sharp-pointed. Those spines which support fins are never branched.

Spinule: a small spine. Term generally not used in reference to the small spines of fins.

Standard length: the length of a fish from the front of the upper lip to the posterior end of the vertebral column (the last element of which, the hypural plate, is somewhat broadened and forms the bony support for the caudal fin rays).

Stripe: a horizontal straight-sided color marking.

Subopercle: an elongate flat dermal bone which is one of the four comprising the operculum; lies below the opercle and forms the ventro-posterior margin of the operculum.

Suborbital: in reference to the region below the eye or to the series of bones rimming the lower margin of the orbit of a fish.

Subspecies: a geographical variant of a species; the subspecific name is the third part of a trinomial name of an organism.

Substratum: a stratum or layer lying under another; in the sea often used in reference to the bottom.

Suture: an immovable articulation of two bones.

Swim bladder: a tough-walled gas-filled sac lying in the upper part of the body cavity of many bony fishes just beneath the vertebral column, the principal function of which is to offset the weight of the heavier tissues, particularly bone. The organ is also called the air bladder or the gas bladder.

Symphysis: an articulation, generally immovable, between two bones; often used in reference to the anterior region of juncture of the two halves of the jaws.

Synonym: an invalid scientific name resulting from the earlier naming (and description) of the same organism.

Tail: that part of a fish posterior to the anus.

Teleost: refers to the Teleostei, the highest superorder of the ray-fin bony fishes, including all those of the present book. The others are the Chondrostei (the sturgeons and paddlefishes are the living representatives) and Holostei (the bowfin and gars are the contemporary forms). The Teleostei and Holostei may be polyphyletic (of multiple origin), so these superordinal group names, though often heard, are usually omitted from recent formal classifications.

Terminal phase: the second color phase, always male, of a sexually dichromatic fish such as a wrasse or parrotfish; the result of a change of sex of an initial-phase female.

Thoracic: referring to the chest region.

Thorax: the chest region of the body of a fish, hence ventrally between the head and abdomen.

Total length: the length of a fish from the front of whichever jaw is most anterior to the end of the longest caudal ray.

Transformation: a radical change in the form of an organism during development over a relatively short period of time; in fishes this refers to the morphological change from the postlarval (or prejuvenile) stage to the juvenile.

Trifid: branched into three approximately equal parts; usually used in reference to the divided end of a cirrus or tooth.

Trunk: the part of the body of a fish anterior to the anus (excluding the head).

Truncate: square-ended; used to describe a caudal fin with a vertically straight terminal border and angular or slightly rounded corners.

Tubefeet: small, slender, extensible, sucker-tipped projections which provide for the locomotion of echinoderm animals such as starfishes and sea urchins.

Tunicate: an invertebrate marine animal of the phylum Chordata, subphylum Tunicata, characterized by a tough flexible outer tunic and a tadpole-like larval form with a structural notochord in the tail. Simple sessile adults (called sea squirts) have two external openings permitting the circulations of water through a sievelike internal branchial sac. Tunicates may be pelagic or benthic, solitary or colonial.

Upper limb: refers either to the vertical free margin of the preopercle or to the number of gill rakers on the first gill arch above the angle.

Ventral: of or pertaining to the lower part of an animal; the opposite of dorsal.

Vertical scale rows: the near-vertical rows of scales between the upper end of the gill opening and base of caudal fin; sometimes called the lateral scale rows.

Villiform: like the villi of the intestine, hence with numerous small slender projections. Used to describe bands of small close-set teeth, particularly if slender. If the teeth are short, they are often termed cardiform.

Vomer: a median unpaired bone toward the front of the roof of the mouth, the anterior end of which often bears teeth.

Zoanthid: a member of the anthozoan coelenterate order Zoanthidea; there is no calcareous skeleton, and the polyps are usually joined together at the base for form a colony.

Zooplankton: the animals of the plankton.